Midland
Murders & Mysteries

by Barrie Roberts

*QuercuS

****
QuercuS
John Roberts
8 Hillside Close, Bartley Green
Birmingham B32 4LT
****

Midland Murders & Mysteries

by Barrie Roberts

ISBN 1 898136 14 9

First Published 1997

Preface

QuercuS specialises in publishing books about the western Midlands, or the area between the rivers Trent, Severn and Avon that geographers call the "Midland Triangle". Titles include *Midland Woods & Forests, Midland Rivers, Midland Ghosts & Hauntings, Midland Castles, Historic Houses & Gardens, Heart in my Boots, Coaching Days in the Midlands* and sets of pen and ink sketches of buildings in Hales Owen, Bromserove and Birmingham. Coming soon are *Midland Spirits & Spectres* and *Us Kids*.

Barrie Roberts was one of the authors of our first *Ghosts* book, called in as an expert to comment on the stories. Realising his interest in (and considerable knowledge of) matters mysterious and sinister, I asked him to write this book.

The Author

BARRIE ROBERTS was born in Hampshire in 1939, but has made his home in the Midlands for over thirty years. For most of that period he worked in criminal law for two firms of solicitors, working on a number of murder cases, major frauds and the appeals of the Birmingham Six.

He is now a legal consultant and internationally published writer. His books include *Sherlock Holmes and the Railway Maniac* (1994), *Sherlock Holmes and the Devil's Grail* (1995) and the soon forthcoming *Sherlock Holmes and the Man from Hell*. He was the cooauthor (with Anne Bradford) of *Midland Ghosts & Hauntings* (QuercuS 1994), to which a sequel *Midland Spirits & Spectres* is to be published in late 1997.

Barrie is a lecturer for the City of Birmingham, teaching courses at Great Barr on "Ghosts & Unsolved Mysteries".

Apart from his professional involvement with the law Barrie is a lifelong collector of accounts of crime cases, and these cases come largely from his huge private library.

Sources and Acknowledgements

There is a great accumulation of books and cuttings about past murders in my own library. However, for those who cannot spare forty years to make such a collection, let me name some other sources used in this book.

No writer on murder can ever ignore the work of those who have gone before, and I take this opportunity to acknowledge the help received from Michael Posner's *Midland Murders* (Star Publications, 1973), Betty Smith's *Warwickshire Murders* (Countryside Books, 1991), W M Jamieson's *Murders, Myths and Monuments of North Staffordshire* (Westmid Supplies, 1979), and Brian Lane's *The Murder Club Guide to the Midlands* (Harrap, 1988). In all of them you will find Midland cases which I have not included.

It is impossible to research the past of the West Midlands without recourse to twenty five years' issues of the *Black Country Bugle*, a publication which indefatigably hunts the stories of old crimes in its area and often inspires readers to supply personal recollections and old documents.

The Public Libraries of the region are too many to mention, but I refer you to them, particularly Birmingham Reference Library and the Salt Library at Stafford. I refer you also to the West Midlands Police Museum at Birmingham.

Where a Midland murder has attracted national attention, I have sometimes turned to the *Notable British Trials* series and to the Penguin *Famous Trials*. At a more local level, I must thank ex Detective Sergeant Pat Gavin for drawing my attention to the Cattle Bridge murder at Rushall and the Rushall Museum Newsletter of Manor Farm Community School for further details.

Finally, I must thank my brother, the military historian Phillip Roberts, for his considerable help with the story of Captain Roy Farran and the murder of his brother.

Barrie Roberts
1997

Contents

NB. These locations are given with their counties at the relevant date to explain, for example, why a Dudley crime was tried at Worcester.

Introduction

Anyone who adventures into writing about true crimes will
soon realise that he stands last in a long list. The honours
of it are many and must go to such as Thomas de Quincey,
William Bolitho, F Tennyson Jesse and Eric Ambler. The
dishonours are more numerous and widely known, including
the 18th and 19th century broadsheet writers, the sanctim-
onious hacks of publications like *The Newgate Calendar* and
God's Vengeance Upon Murder Discovered, and sensationalist
scribblers of the popular press from the *Illustrated Police
News* down to today.

If I cannot count myself a star of the genre, I hope that in
making this collection I have not stumbled into the gutter.
There are people who believe the public interest in crime is
depraved, and that its prominence in England is evidence of
something rotten in our society. They point to the groaning
shelves of books and magazines dealing with murder in fact
and fiction, as though it were pornography. They should
instead boast, as we can, that England's murder rate is the
lowest in the western world, so low compared to other
allegedly civilised nations as to be inexplicable. One explanation may be that we have a very long established rule
of law, whereas the USA is little more than a century
from frontier days and our European neighbours have
mostly suffered recent revolutions and invasions.

Maybe that is right, but whatever the cause, our slender
murder rate and our enormous interest in the subject seem
contradictory. Perhaps it is because we have been so successful in suppressing the murderer within us all that we
view, with more intense curiosity, the few who do break
the ultimate law of God and man. Eric Ambler said that
"There is a criminal and a policeman inside every human
being", but William Bolitho went further:

> "The theatre may rival in the hands of a genius the
> naive drama of the courts, though in England at any
> rate the theatre has dilapidated itself in trying to make
> our ethics plausible, and the "real-life" drama has
> no serious rival. But it is its reality, not its drama,
> wherein lies the core of the interest in murder. We

have a need for the sight of life - and death as for
salt. We wage slaves live continually in incompletion
and inexplicability; we strain for a sight of stars and
mud; we wish to take our bearings and know where
we stand."

So be it. This collection then, is for those who wish to take
their bearings by the deeds and fate of others. If it draws
its material only from the English Midlands that is not a
fault. The most common British murder is undistinguished,
involving a friend or relative, most often a spouse, cracking
under some real or imagined strain and applying a rolling pin
or a carving knife. They do not make interesting reading. In
any region of England one must be selective and try to recall
de Quincey's classic definition:

"Design, gentlemen, grouping, light and shade, poetry,
sentiment are now deemed indispensable to attempts of
this nature."

The varied landscape, rich history and polyglot population
that has made the Midlands has, I hope, left us enough
murders that hold some spark of interest for the reader.
Some of the cases are quite well known, many are not;
some were solved, some were not. All occurred more
than thirty years ago, a limit applied because I am not
interested in disturbing the grief of survivors, nor in
retelling recent tales that are still well remembered.

If this collection of Midland murders from the 18th to the
20th century fails to please, do not blame the murderers for
lack of drama or poetry, light or shade. The only possible
suspect is myself.

There's No Copper Big Enough
(Willenhall, Staffs 1864/5)

Popular belief holds that when a police officer is murdered
his colleagues never rest until they obtain a conviction for
the crime. Modern cases tend to confirm this, but consider
what happened in Willenhall a hundred and thiry years ago,
when not one, but two officers were killed.

Like all the industrial towns of the area, Willenhall grew up
on coal and iron, but it developed into the world centre of
lock making. It also developed a reputation as a violent
town; at one time its citizens were barred from the market
in nearby Walsall.

Helping to uphold the law in 19th Century Willenhall was
PC Enoch Augustus Hooper, a bachelor in his early thirties
who had been a Staffordshire County Police officer since
1856. After seven years at Darlaston he transferred to Willenhall in 1863. He had a reputation as a quiet man who
preferred reason to the truncheon and the handcuffs, but
was quite able to respond to unreasonable people.

Just after 11 pm on Saturday 7th May 1864, Hooper was on
patrol when he was called by PC Dutton to help a third officer who was under attack. The embattled constable was 21
year old William Lyons, a man known to be overfond of the
truncheon. Outside the Hope & Anchor pub Lyons had met a
group of drunks, one of whom, George Lockley, had felt the
weight of Lyons' truncheon before and resented it.

Lockley and a friend ignored the officer's commands to move
on. Instead they followed him along his beat, shouting abuse.
When Lyons threatened arrests, Lockley struck him and John
Edwards joined in. At this point Lyons was not in difficulty
and had nearly handcuffed Lockley, when the odds changed.
Lockley's brother Tom, Joseph Willetts and Joshua Stanley
arrived and joined the fight. Soon Lyons was on the ground,
being kicked about the head.

A bystander, William Lowe, dragged one of the attackers
away, PCs Hooper and Dutton arrived, and all might have
been well had not one of the attackers snatched up a large
stone and smashed it into Lyons' face. The five hooligans

were arrested and Lyons was carried, unconscious, into a nearby house.

The Lockleys and their companions were still remanded in custody awaiting trial for assault and public disorder on May 18th when PC Lyons died, apparently from a fractured skull caused by the blow from a stone. Now the defendants were charged with murder and Willenhall began to contemplate a five man hanging at Stafford.

The Assize came to Stafford within weeks and few doubted that some, if not all, of the defendants would hang as a warning that attacks on police officers would not be tolerated. Instead, the judge suggested to the jury that there was no proof of murderous intent and no certainty as to who had struck with the stone. Verdicts of manslaughter were given and the five villains were sentenced to prison for between two and five years. Robbed of its sensation, Willenhall turned back to lockmaking and drinking, but its police officers were dumbfounded.

Eighteen months after Lyons' death, PC Hooper was again on patrol when trouble flared at a pub. On the bitterly cold night of 8th December 1865, PC William Butler went to deal with a row at the Royal George in Walsall Street.

Landlord Thomas Williams was in difficulties with four Irish men who were refusing to leave. They pleaded that one of them, Patsy Cane alias Patsy Rowan, had nowhere to sleep that night and argued for the use of one of the inn's bedrooms. Cane was well drunk, Williams refused and the loud row which followed attracted PC Butler's attention.

Butler entered the pub, sized up the situation, and ordered the four out. Cane was for making a fight of it, but his companions pulled him away. As he went he snarled at Butler "There's no copper in Willenhall big enough to take me!"

Butler was an experienced officer who must have heard many drunken threats, and Cane's abuse did not stop him from leaving the Royal George ten minutes later. He continued on his beat, across Walsall Street to Bilston Street and up past the Railway Tavern. Beside the Railway Tavern lay a narrow, unpaved way called Love Alley, leading to a row of five slum cottages.

As he reached the mouth of Love Alley the four Irishmen leapt out at him. Drawing his truncheon he gave as good as he got and soon the noise of the scrap brought PC Hooper from his beat. The two of them were soon winning the fight, but reinforcements joined the attackers in the shape of Patrick Cane and his partly deaf wife, Mary. Residents of one of the cottages on Love Alley, they were also Irish, though not related to Patsy Cane.

The noise of the enlarged battle began to wake neighbours. John Whitehouse and Henry Benton watched from the windows of Love Alley cottages, while Charles Smith left his house on the other side of Bilston Street to get a better view. John Ward, licensee of the Railway Tavern, looked out of his kitchen window, and two neighbours, Charles Reynolds and David Richards, went to the alley's mouth.

Suddenly a shout of "Murder!" brought the fight to an end. The attackers paused and PC Hooper was seen on the ground. Only now did the onlookers go to help the police, causing the attackers to flee except for John McCue, who had been stunned by Butler's truncheon.

Superintendent Oswell and Inspector Thompson arrived quickly, with Dr Pitt, but Hooper was dead. The battered PC Butler insisted on taking part in the hot pursuit of his friend's murderer and said that Hooper had gone at Patrick Cane with his truncheon, that they had grappled and fallen to the ground and that Cane had drawn a long knife from his coat and stabbed Hooper in the chest. He specifically recalled that Hooper had risen, clutched at his chest, staggered a few paces and then dropped.

The civilian witnesses were not much help. Smith agreed with PC Butler but had been some distance away, while the remainder could not remember seeing Hooper and Cane struggling. Even so, acting on Butler's account the police arrived on Patrick Cane's doorstep within minutes.

Mary Cane was still up, but Patrick was in bed. Both denied any part in Hooper's death. Examination of the cottage revealed blood spots on Cane's clothing and boots, and on the front door knob. Bloody hand prints showed on the stair banister and a knife was missing from the carving set in the kitchen. Husband and wife were arrested and charged with murder.

An inquest at the Neptune Inn also found that Patrick Cane had murdered the officer and sent him and his wife for trial at Stafford Assizes.

Patrick McCue, who was known to have been unconscious when PC Hooper was stabbed, came before the magistrates on a charge of assaulting PC Butler and was fined £10. John Leonard, fourth member of the original ambush, was not prosecuted.

The Canes' trial took place at the Spring Assize at Stafford in March 1866. In the so called Crown Court of Stafford's ancient Court House, they stood before Mr Justice Montague Smith, a man with a reputation for fair but speedy trials.

Prosecution barrister McMahon knew that his case was weak. While PC Butler's account of the stabbing would be supported by the civilian Smith, the defence would inevitably produce those witnesses who never saw Hooper and Cane struggle. In addition, there was no evidence whatsoever of Mary Cane's involvement in the murder, only that she helped her husband later. In fact, she had probably been charged only to prevent her giving evidence for Patrick under the law then in force.

The case was shorter than anyone had expected, even before Montague Smith. Late in the morning Dr Pitt came to the witness box and testified that the stabbing had been so violent that the knife had passed through PC Hooper's lung and damaged his spine. It was at this point that the case fell apart. Defence counsel, Mr Young, asked the crucial question;

> Young: "And how far would the officer have been able to stagger after receiving such a wound?"

> Dr Pitt: "He wouldn't. He wouldn't have been able to rise from the ground. The damage to his spine would have paralysed him."

Dr Pitt had inflicted a fatal wound to the prosecution case. After a discussion with the Judge, McMahon offered no further evidence and the Jury were directed to acquit both defendants. Wasting no time, the Canes went home, packed and vanished from Willenhall.

The police were appalled. Two officers had been murdered on duty with no murder conviction and only a £10 fine in the second case. A hunt began for the other Canes, Patsy and Edward, who had disappeared after the killing, but they were never found.

The murders of PC Lyons and PC Hooper remain, officially, unsolved. Lyons died at the hand of a local man and it is not impossible that somebody somewhere knows that his great-grandfather murdered him. What of PC Hooper? If Dr Pitt was right in his opinion, then PC Butler could not have been accurate in his evidence. If Butler was wrong and Patrick Cane did not stab the officer, who did? The bloodstains and the missing knife point to someone in the Cane household. Was it, by any chance, Mary Cane?

What's Your Poison?
(Rugeley, Staffs 1894)

The time worn drinkers' cliche of the title is said by some to have originated in Staffordshire pubs 140 years ago, as a sardonic comment on the career of a local doctor.

Sherlock Holmes believed that when doctors turned to crime they had "nerve and knowledge". Dr William Palmer had both, but not sufficient to save him from two other aspects of his personality, naivety and nastiness.

The son of a wealthy timber merchant who died unexpect-edly, leaving no will, Palmer stood to inherit £7,000 on his majority under an arrangement made by his elder brother. His prospects made the young apprentice surgeon attractive to women, including one determined redhead, but a wealthy future depended on him not doing anything to displease his brother, including marrying young.

Balked of her expectations, the redhead announced that she was pregnant and needed £50 to pay an abortionist. When Palmer was unable to finance the operation the lady disapp-eared, returning to announce that she had made her own arrangements and now needed £200 because she had been forced to ask the abortionist for credit.

ILLUSTRATED AND UNABRIDGED EDITION
OF

The ☙ Times

REPORT

OF THE

TRIAL OF WILLIAM PALMER,

FOR POISONING JOHN PARSONS COOK,

AT RUGELEY.

THE TALBOT ARMS, RUGELEY, THE SCENE OF COOK'S DEATH.

FROM THE SHORT-HAND NOTES TAKEN IN THE CENTRAL CRIMINAL COURT
FROM DAY TO DAY.

LONDON: WARD AND LOCK, 158, FLEET STREET.
1856.

That abortionists have never been famous for giving credit never occurred to young Palmer. Faced with the loss of his inheritance he first tried betting to raise the money. When that failed he began stealing from his employers. He made the necessary sum but was soon dismissed under a cloud, his doting mother making good the firm's losses.

His red headed friend still had her sights on him and in her next move, lured him away to an inn at Walsall where he was unable to meet the bill. His brother heard what was happening, descended on Walsall and caught the couple. William returned to Rugeley in disgrace and the lady cut her losses, married another and sailed for Australia.

Medical studies in London followed, where the student surgeon took a full account of the capital's opportunities for loose and high living before returning to Rugeley and setting up in practice. As a newly qualified surgeon now in receipt of his inheritance he seemed to have a rosy future.

Alas, his inheritance had long been pledged to money lenders to cover his mounting debts, and his reputation as a seducer of young women was spreading, coupled with stories of at least four illegitimate children. To meet his debts he was borrowing money against acceptances forged in his mother's name, letting her pay his creditors when they fell due. At this unpropitious point he married.

Palmer's wife also had an unusual history, being the illegitimate daughter of a retired East India Company officer and his housekeeper. Her father's "suicide" had been sufficiently unusual to place her mother under threat of the gallows, from which she had escaped through the combination of an inventive doctor and a gullible Coroner's Court.

Palmer's mother in law took to the bottle, who can blame her, and after an attack of delirium tremens was taken to the surgeon's home where he nursed her personally until she died.

The hard pressed surgeon continued his destructive gambling and forgery, but also insured his wife's life for £13,000; he tried for £25,000 but one company refused the proposal.

The death of his heavily insured wife in 1854 rescued him again, but not for long. His surgical practice now virtually non existent, he divided his activities between gambling, borrowing money, forgery, raising race horses and poisoning. Now to the rumours of his debts and his sex life were added speculations about deaths associated with him. A man called Abley, husband of a lady on whom Palmer had cast his eye, died suddenly after a drinking bout with the surgeon. An awkward patient and one of Palmer's illegitimate children died. A man named Bladon called on Palmer, having told his wife that he expected to collect several hundred pounds from him. Persuaded to stay in Rugeley, the visitor fell mysteriously ill and died. Only £150 was found among his effects but, when the widow challenged Palmer with owing her husband money, that gentleman said that the truth was the opposite, though he would never have referred to her husband's debt if she had not raised the matter.

A proposal to insure the life of an alcoholic brother, Walter, was rejected by several insurers, if only because he was already suffering from bouts of delirium tremens, but was eventually accepted at £14,000. Given a credit account for gin at an inn in Dudley Port by his amiable brother, Walter Palmer soon drank himself into the grave. Unhappily for Palmer, a suspicious doctor wrote to the Prince of Wales Assurance Company who withheld payment.

In desperation Palmer applied to Walter's widow to pay sums which he claimed his late brother had owed him, but the ruse failed. Meanwhile a number of assurance companies were comparing information and investigating William Palmer of Rugeley.

Matters came to a head in 1855 after the November races at Shrewsbury. John Parsons Cook, a solicitor friend of Palmer, had a successful meeting because his horse *Polestar* won the Shrewsbury Handicap. Palmer and Cook were cronies, Cook having stood as a referee when Palmer made an unsuccessful attempt to insure the life of a local farmer. When at the celebration of his Shrewsbury success he fell suddenly sick, Cook voiced his suspicions of the surgeon and tried to keep his winnings out of Palmer's hands.

Cook died at Rugeley's Talbot Arms Hotel and his cash winnings and betting book were stolen by his erstwhile friend, now driven to recklessness by the failure of his investment in brother Walter. Armed with a forged authority Palmer collected Cook's winnings at Tattersalls and generously arranged the solicitor's funeral, having made some £5,000 by poisoning his friend.

Nerve, knowledge and nastiness had carried Palmer through the years; he was betrayed by his naivety in believing that a town as small as Rugeley could ignore his activities. Cook's family and the assurance company investigators heard the gossip in Rugeley. A postmortem on Cook was demanded and, in its wake, the deadly doctor was arrested.

Although he was charged only with the murder of Cook, all of Staffordshire suspected him of multiple poisoning and looked forward to a spectacular trial, but they were disappointed. It was argued on his behalf that local prejudice against him was so strong as to make a fair trial at Stafford impossible. True or not, the argument was accepted and a special Act of Parliament passed to transfer proceedings to the Old Bailey.

The trial opened on 14th May 1856 before Lord Chief Justice Campbell, Mr Justice Cresswell and Baron Alderson. Sitting with them were the Lord Mayor, two Sheriffs, two Under Sheriffs and seven Aldermen. One of them was Alderman Sidney, a native of Rugeley and former MP for Stafford. The Alderman's descendants were to become the centre of a poisoning scandal that rocked Croydon in the 1920s and remains officially unsolved. Competition for public seats was fierce, and among the spectators was Lord Lucan, of Crimean War fame, one of whose descendants was to kill his childrens' nanny and flee Britain.

Attorney General Cockburn prosecuted (a sure mark of official determination to obtain a conviction) and Mr Serjeant Shee defended, briefed by Birmingham's famous solicitor "Honest John" Smith. Among the Juniors for the Prosecution was Mr Huddleston who, as a Judge three decades later would try the "Mignonette" cannibals. A Junior barrister on the defence team was Mr Kenealey, whose defence in 1874 of Arthur Orton, the Tichborne claimant, led to his censure by the Bar.

This star studded cast was supported over fourteen days of the trial by a procession of gentleman, doctors, Professors of Medicine and chambermaids. Lord Chief Justice Campbell prosecuted at least as effectively as the Attorney General, while the Police took potential defence witnesses to remote places, away from solicitor Smith's enquiry agents; all this to bolster a case whose central weakness was the inability of the Prosecution to prove poisoning. Professor Taylor opined that Palmer had weakened Cook with anti-mony and then finished the job with strychnine, but had to admit that a human body could absorb up to sixty grains of

antimony, a constituent of the stock remedy tartar emetic.
Where strychnine was concerned he had the advantage of
knowing that Palmer had purchased strychnine, but had
found none in his examinations. A press poet commented:

> In antimony, great though his faith,
> The quantity found being small,
> Taylor's faith in strychnine was yet greater,
> For of that he found nothing at all.

Nevertheless, despite the varied opinions of seven medical
men for the Prosecution and eleven for the Defence, the Jury
took only an hour and a quarter to return a guilty verdict.
As the Judge passed sentence of death, Palmer scribbled a
note and tossed it to his solicitor, "It was the riding that
did it", a rueful gambler's tribute to a winning jockey. The
Lord Chief Justice had certainly applied the whip skilfully
during the trial.

Public and scientific debate raged after the verdict. It was
the first time that strychnine poisoning had been alleged in
a murder trial and Palmer's solicitor tried to obtain a new
examination of Cook's remains. He pleaded with the Home
Secretary that concealment of evidence by the Crown and
the Judge's misdirection of the Jury, the disputed medical
evidence and the disappearance of Defence witnesses should
lead to a reprieve. He was unsuccessful.

If Staffordshire had been disappointed to lose the trial, it
took full advantage of the execution. On Saturday 14th June,
as the County Police and one hundred and fifty Special Constables patrolled the streets, thousands of spectators swarmed
into Stafford. Stands had been erected around the gallows
and the roofs of nearby houses boarded over to provide
vantage points.

Seats were selling as high as a guinea each. One hundred
thousand people had come to see the finish of Billy Palmer's
last race.

The show was a brief one. Hangman Smith of Dudley who,
apart from his rare profession, claimed the distinction of
having been jailed for racing naked through the streets of
Wednesbury, appeared with the condemned man. The huge
crowd may have expected some such sporty comment from
Palmer as that with which he had received the verdict,

but it was not to be. Palmer prayed briefly, shook hands with Smith and said "God bless you!" as the trap dropped beneath him.

Rugeley cringed under the national ill fame that the case had attracted. Through the good offices of Alderman Sidney, the burghers of the town obtained an interview with the Prime Minister, seeking his support for an attempt to change the town's name. He agreed promptly, provided that the town was named after him - Palmerston.

So Rugeley it remains. Palmer lies in Stafford Gaol, but Cook's grave may be seen in St Augustine's churchyard. The Talbot Arms has become the Shrewsbury Arms and Palmer's old surgery across the street is now a shop. The poisoner's only surviving son committed suicide in 1925.

The West Bromwich Tragedy
(West Bromwich, Staffs 1894)

Victorian England had a popular press fully as lurid as anything we have today, if not more so. The coming of rotary presses and the abolition of Stamp Duty on newspapers lead to the first tabloids. *The Illustrated Police News* and *The Illustrated Police Budget* were decried from pulpits and sneered at by the middle class for their lurid illustrations and their devotion to murder, suicide, disaster and sex, but the recipe worked. Mockingly called "The slavey's Bible", the *Illustrated Police Budget* turned the insult on its head and urged readers to "Kindly Throw Your Copy of IPB Down an Area. It will Brighten the Slavey's Long Hour of Toil." [Area - a front, basement level yard.]

It was the *Budget* that seized on an obscure crime in West Bromwich and headlined it as "The West Bromwich Tragedy".

One day in June 1894 Major Hassall returned from work to his father's home at 31 Herbert Street in West Bromwich. Though the kitchen was as he had left it in the morning, the sitting room door was locked.

Borrowing a neighbour's ladder, he climbed up to a window and saw:

From the "Illustrated Police Budget" of June 1894

Mrs Hall (his father's housekeeper) lying across the foot of the bed. Witness told his brother that he had better fetch a policeman. There was a large quantity of blood on the bed. Sergeant Owen came and burst the door open, and found Mrs Hall was dead.

Sergeant Owen told the Inquest how he went to Mr Hassall's bedroom and found the latter lying face down by the bed. He was wearing only trousers and stockings and was also dead. A carving knife lay by the dead man's side and it seemed that Hassall had cut his throat while sitting on a chair.

Major Hassall deposed that his father had been depressed and found work difficult; he had an abscess on his neck occasioned by an explosion at his house and, thirteen years earlier, had blown off one of his great toes with a gun.

Dr Manley said that Mrs Hall's windpipe was severed and there were slight cuts on the back of her left hand. There were two deep cuts on the inner side of her right index finger. Her death was caused by the throat wound, which he thought could not have been self inflicted and had been made from behind. Mrs Hall had been fully dressed apart from her bodice and among the articles in her pockets were her bedroom doorkey, 8s 6d (42.5p) in coins and a religious tract called *"Sold Under Sin"*. In Hassall's pockets were 19s 11 1/2d (99.5p) and an ordinary pocket knife.

The Coroner's Jury managed to ignore the vast possibilities of the evidence, and quickly returned a verdict of wilful murder against Hassall and that he committed suicide while in a state of temporary insanity. The lurid spotlight of the *Illustrated Police Budget* turned to other subjects and Herbert Street sank back into obscurity, leaving the thoughtful to wonder.

Why was Hassall only partly dressed? Why was Mrs Hall without her bodice? If she had the bedroom key in her pocket, how did Hassall get in? Why was the money in Hassall's pocket 1/2d short of a pound? Was the missing halfpenny the price of the religious tract? Was the tract significant? What really happened between the depressive Mr Hassall and his housekeeper?

Cannot Come Tonight
(Worcester 1925)

When Florence Hardwick arrived at her workplace at 7 o'clock on the morning of 27th November 1925, she opened the outer door with her own key so as not to wake her employer Ernest Laight, landlord of Worcester's Garibaldi Inn.

Once inside the pub, she was surprised to find the inner door unlocked, the bar door and windows unlocked, the kitchen door open and the pub's back door wide open.

Calling her employers' names she moved through the building, wondering uneasily why there was no reply. Upstairs she found that the Laights' bed had not been slept in, baby Robert lay in his cot and in the next room little Joan Laight was in bed, asleep.

Thoroughly frightened by her knowledge that Ernie and Doris Laight would not have left their children alone, Mrs Hardwick went out and accosted a local insurance agent, Danny Oram, who suggested they search the pub together. Behind the bar the floor was scattered with copper coins and tokens from slot machines. Oram lifted the cellar trap. A smell of burning emerged and he descended to find the bodies of Ernest and Doris Laight. Paper had been piled on Doris' skirt and set alight, apparently in an attempt to burn the bodies, if not the pub.

Oram asked Mrs Hardwick to fetch the Police and went upstairs. There he found that Joan was still asleep but Robert was dead. Police officers arrived and established that the bar till had been rifled, a cash box upstairs emptied and another forced and robbed of all but 7s 6d (37.5p). Dr Simmons came and examined the bodies, revealing that the Laights had been shot but little Bobby had been struck with a blunt instrument.

Through the November morning the grim news spread across Worcester. About 7.45 am PC William Devey was on duty at the Cross and met a colleague who asked him,

"Have you heard of the affair at the Garibaldi Inn? Ern Laight and his wife have been shot. I was the last one with them. I'm supposed to be going on leave today. Do you think this will prevent me going?"

Detective Sergeant Fisher had returned from the Garibaldi when he met Devey, who repeated to him the odd questions of Probationer Constable Herbert Burrowes. Fisher knew it was after 9.00 am when Dr Simmons had said that the Laights had been shot.

PC Burrowes was on his beat early that afternoon when he received a message to report to Headquarters. Questioned by Fisher, he said that he had heard about the Laights being shot at about 8.00 am. He was ordered to remain at the Police Station while Fisher and others took the keys to his lodgings at 92 Wyld's Lane.

Searching the probationer's lodgings they found a five shot revolver, 36 live rounds and three empty cartridge cases. They also found in a suitcase packed with clothes, 34 £1 banknotes, 26 ten shilling (50p) notes, £22 8s (22.40p) in silver and a mounted gold sovereign. There were slot machine tokens on the floor.

By 4.15 pm they had returned to the Station, where Burrowes was shown the items found and charged with all three murders. He made a brief statement:

I voluntarily and freely admit that I killed at 12.50 am on November 27th, Mr Laight and Mrs Laight and Robert Laight. The cause will remain unknown. I apologise to the officers and men of the Worcester City Police for the disgrace incurred.

He also managed to send a telegram to his parents, who had been expecting him home on leave that night:

"Cannot come tonight. Letter following, explaining. Love, Bob."

His home was in Middle Road, East Barnet, London and his stepfather was a recently retired Acting Sergeant of the Metropolitan Police. Herbert (or Bob) Burrowes had joined the Worcester City Force nine months earlier after some years at sea.

On 4th December Worcester City Magistrates heard the
evidence. Bullets taken from the Laights had been matched
with Burrowes' pistol. A brewery accountant deposed that
the average weekly takings of the Garibaldi were about £30
and, the pub's account having been last settled on November
9th, there should have been some £89 there in cash. The
money in Burrowes' bedroom totalled £69/8s (£69.40p) and
he had £18/5s/6d (£18.27.5p) on him, a total of £87/13s/
6d (£87.67.5p)

Dr Simmons confirmed his earlier conclusions and PC
Devey gave evidence of his conversations with Burrowes,
at the Cross and later at breakfast in the Police Station.
Detective Sergeant Fisher told of his questioning Burrowes,
who said that both the Laights had wished him "Goodnight"
as he left the Garibaldi and that he had heard of the kill-
ings from a man in Lowesmoor about 8.00 in the morning.
Fisher also reported finding moneylenders' receipts in the
probationer's room. Mrs Gertrude Griffiths, sister of Doris
Laight, wept as she identified the sovereign found in Burrowes' room as one of two that her late father had given to
her and her sister. Burrowes was committed for trial.

Despite the overwhelming case against him, when his trial
opened at Worcester Assizes on 27th January 1926 Burrowes
pleaded not guilty to all three charges. The only possible
defence was insanity, and his Counsel set about establishing
it. However, although Burrowes' medical record from the
Navy showed that he suffered from hereditary syphilis, and
although the medical witnesses could agree that this led to
insanity in many cases, no doctor would say that Burrowes
actually showed signs of insanity. Meanwhile the Prosecutor
emphasised the way in which Burrowes, a friend of the
Laights, had gone to the Garibaldi with a pistol and rubber
gloves and had stayed there for an hour and a half, seemingly cheerful but actually waiting his chance to kill and
steal. This was not, they claimed, the conduct of a lunatic,
but of a cold, calculating killer. In vain the Defence argued
that the murders were themselves the symptom of Burrowes'
degeneration into insanity. The Jury took thirty seven
minutes to convict on all three counts.

Burrowes made no appeal and refused to see visitors during
his last twenty two days of life. This "cold-blooded brute"
did, however, perform one act of decency from the condemned cell. He wrote to a friend of the Laights:

"For yours, and Joan's sake, I wish to deny the rumour that has been circulating through Worcester and elsewhere, to the effect that there was any intimacy between Mrs Laight and I.

She was a good and respectable woman, and was respected by myself, as well as others who knew her. There was absolutely no truth whatever in the rumour, and in my opinion it was circulated by people who had nothing better to do.

If you wish to publish this denial, please do so.

If you can - forgive me, for I am sorry."

With that off his chest Burrowes passed his days singing and playing cards until 17th February 1926, when he ate a hearty breakfast and stepped out of his cell at Gloucester to be hanged. He lies near the prison's north wall, next to Major Armstrong, the solicitor who poisoned his wife in 1922.

Was he insane? Today he would probably have been found so. No hidden cause for the murders has ever come to light. His debts were not excessive. He was engaged to marry in a few weeks, but that was hardly a motive. He told his stepfather it was robbery.

She's in Pieces
(Hednesford, Staffs 1919)

Lizzie Talbot married Harry Gaskin in 1913. With the outbreak of the Great War, Gaskin was among the first from the little mining village of Hednesford, Staffordshire, to volunteer for the Army.

Unlike many volunteers and conscripts of the Great War, Harry came home unscathed, though he had spent two and a half years in the trenches of the Western Front. Friends gave him a huge homecoming party when he returned in January 1919, but Lizzie was, perhaps, less than welcoming. During his long absence she had borne two children, neither fathered by her husband.

The village considered Lizzie a slut and Harry agreed. Very shortly after his return from the war, they separated and she went to live with her mother, Mrs Emily Talbot, at 72 Brindley Heath.

Just before 2 pm on 19th February 1919, Mrs Talbot had a visitor. He was Tom Saunders, a stoker at West Cannock Colliery where Harry Gaskin now worked. He said that he had met Harry in the Anglesey Arms, after his shift, and Harry had asked him to deliver a note to Lizzie. The note said:

"Meet me round the pool at once - Important."

Leaving the note on the hall table, Lizzie put on her hat and coat and went out into the cold, grey afternoon.

By the early February nightfall she had not returned. By 11 pm Mrs Talbot was frantic. Next morning, with no sign of Lizzie, she went to see Gaskin where he lived in Bridgtown, Cannock.

He denied seeing Lizzie on the previous day, though he admitted he had intended to see her and tell her he was getting a divorce. Emily Talbot hurried to Hednesford Police Station and reported her daughter missing.

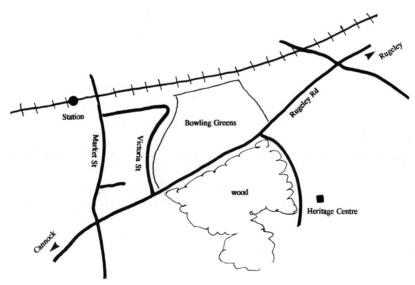

Hednesford today.

Hednesford Police called on Cannock Station and Superintendent Morrey and Inspector Woolley arrived. A search for a missing person was going to be difficult; dark would fall early, and it had started to snow heavily. Nevertheless, the Police began to seek sightings of Lizzie and information about her contacts.

Soon they had both. Two officials from the Cannock & Rugeley Colliery had seen her with a man by Hednesford Pool on the previous afternoon. The couple had been arguing, but they had gone separate ways, the man climbing a fence and vanishing into a copse near the Colliery. They also picked up the gossip about Lizzie and the name of her latest man, Monty Harris.

With the snow deepening and two reasonable suspects, the Police questioned Harris and Gaskin, hoping, no doubt, for a quick confession. Gaskin only told them what he had said to Mrs Talbot. Harris could prove he was not in the area on the previous day.

Now a huge hunt for Lizzie got under way, pairs of policemen trudging the snow clad streets, lanes and woods, using torches as darkness fell. There was still no sign of the missing woman.

On the afternoon of Friday 21st February, Officers Morrey and Woolley decided to back a hunch. As Gaskin came off shift at the Colliery they were waiting to tell him his wife was still missing and to invite him to the police station. At the station he was arrested on suspicion of murder. Next day he was taken before Thomas Mason JP, and formally charged with his wife's murder, but the hunch seemed to have misfired, Gaskin still would not speak.

It was Sunday afternoon when Harry suddenly asked to see Inspector Woolley. The Inspector had gone home, but soon returned. Gaskin said to him,

> "Is it possible for a search to be made for my wife without the people of Hednesford knowing?" Told that it was, he said,

"Well, I will take you and show you where she is. You will want two drags and two men to pull the drags in opposite directions. She is in pieces. I cut her head off and I tried to cut her legs off".

Accompanied by three Sergeants, Woolley and Gaskin set out in a taxi. Gaskin directed them to the Gasworks in Victoria Road and said, "She's there", indicating one of the huge, cylindrical gasholders.

The great upturned drums that stored town gas were once a commonplace of the urban landscape, but they have almost disappeared. They worked on a simple principal, the lower edge of the drum standing in a circular, water-filled slot. As gas was pumped into or out of the container it could rise or fall while remaining gas tight through the water seal at the bottom.

The Police soon dragged the murky, reeking water in the trench and recovered the hideously mutilated body of Elizabeth Gaskin, but not her head. As the search continued at the Gasworks, Gaskin was taken back to his cell and his wife's remains were laid in the mortuary for her poor mother to identify.

Gaskin now began a confession statement. He admitted meeting his wife by the pool intending to discuss their marriage, but an argument developed. Near the copse they had parted and Gaskin had gone into the wood, as the Colliery officials had seen. However, in the wood he met his wife again and the argument was renewed. At last she taunted him that she was going back to Monty Harris. He grasped her by the throat and pushed her down. As they struggled on the ground he took out a knife and stabbed her until she died.

After her death he covered her body with her own coat and left it under bushes in the copse. Later in the afternoon he and his brother went to the cinema in Cannock.

When Mrs Talbot had called on him he decided to dispose of the corpse, and took a wheelbarrow with an axe, some sharp knives and a sack to the wood. He managed to decapitate her, but finding that it took longer than expected went home, intending to finish the job on the next day.

His first interview with the Police disturbed him. He changed his plan and, just as the Police search really got under way, set out again with his barrow. Loading the corpse into it, he had pushed the sack shrouded barrow up Hednesford Hill until he realized that he dare not take it to the hiding place and leave wheel tracks.

Putting the barrow aside, he carried the headless body nearly 100 yards to the Gasworks. Police officers were in the immediate vicinity but, burdened as he was, he slipped through their cordon and reached the far side of the gasholder. There a seven foot fence stood between him and the moat of the gasometer. With a piece of gaspipe that he picked up, he impaled the body lengthwise, lifted it over the fence and dropped it into the water filled trench.

Harry Gaskin must have done sterling service to his country on the Western Front. Such was his nerve and skill that he returned through the Police search line, recovered the head, braved the Police again and dropped the head into the water. That done, he passed through the search a final time, collected his barrow and went home to Bridgtown.

Police found Lizzie's head on the morning of 25th February and, on the same afternoon an Inquest assembled at Cannock Council Offices. In the light of Harry's statement it took little time to return a verdict of wilful murder against him and commit him for trial.

Gaskin's trial at Stafford on July 11th packed the gallery, for there was a great deal of local sympathy for the 25 year old soldier whose life had been wrecked by a promiscuous young woman. The Prosecutor, Mr C K Vachell, warned the jury of the "ferocious detail" he would have to put before them, and Dr Butter described how, in addition to decapitation, the woman's left arm was broken, there were deep gashes across her abdomen, efforts had been made to remove her breasts and legs and a five foot gas pipe thrust into the body through the neck.

After the short trial, the Jury took just over half an hour to find Gaskin guilty. Then he spoke, for the first time at the trial, and said "I did not mean to kill".

In modern times his war experiences and the considerable element of provocation might result in a verdict of manslaughter, but in 1919 he could not be saved from the gallows. Six thousand people signed a petition for him but gained no reprieve, and on 8th August 1919, Henry Gaskin was hanged at Winson Green Prison, Birmingham. He was 25 years old and his wife was 23. Two more victims of the "War to End All Wars".

The cinema still stands in Walsall Road, Cannock. The offices where the inquest met are still there, and so is the copse where the last, fatal argument exploded. It is called Gaskin's Wood; a decent, brave young soldier and miner is remembered only as a murderer and mutilator.

If Things Had Not Cropped Up
(Ettington, Warks 1897)

It is difficult to imagine that William Hooten, the porter at Ettington Station, Warwickshire, had much to occupy his time in 1897. The village lies on the Roman Fosse Way about 6 miles from Stratford upon Avon and the station stood some way out of Ettington. Not a great commuter station, even a century ago, but Victorian private railways were often under-manned and he might well have been in sole charge of the Station. Whatever the case, when a woman asked him to take a box to Drybank Farm for her one day in September 1897, he said that he could not do so until the morning.

He had time enough to notice that she had stepped out of a Second Class carriage carrying a big tin box and a bundle. He also saw that she seemed distressed by his refusal. She told him that she must have the box with her at the farm that night, but seemed to have difficulty in speaking.

When Hooten was unable or unwilling to help, the woman set out on foot with her luggage. Reaching a crossroads, she sat down to rest on a bench. Local carrier John Heritage soon came by with his cart and stopped to speak. He knew her to be Elizabeth Brandish, sister of George Brandish who lived with his wife and eight children at Drybank Farm.

Miss Brandish asked Heritage to carry her to the farm, but he had other deliveries to make. Nevertheless, she climbed up with him and accompanied him until he was able to deliver her with her box and bundle. She stayed with her brother for two days, then left for Clent to take up a nursing appointment.

Elizabeth Brandish, 34 years old and single, was a nurse. She worked casually for various local committees and individuals, nursing the sick, attending confinements and so on. Between jobs she always gravitated to her brother's home at Ettington.

Some time after Elizabeth's visit, the vicar of Ettington received a letter which puzzled him. Written by a couple called Post from Wye, near Ashford, Kent, the letter enquired about a woman named "Mrs Edwards", a nurse who had a brother in Ettington, and asked about her little son.

The reverend gentleman was puzzled by the enquiry, for he knew no one who filled the description. Initially he was inclined to treat it as a mistake, but something prompted him to pass it to the police.

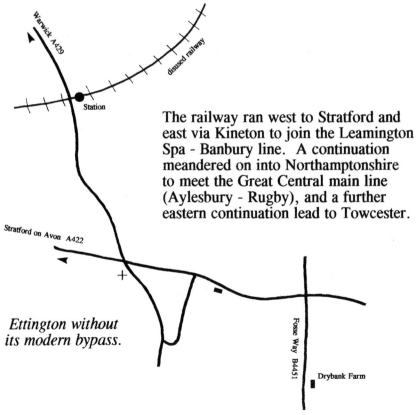

The railway ran west to Stratford and east via Kineton to join the Leamington Spa - Banbury line. A continuation meandered on into Northamptonshire to meet the Great Central main line (Aylesbury - Rugby), and a further eastern continuation lead to Towcester.

Ettington without its modern bypass.

(26)

The police pursued reasonable enquiries; they asked their colleagues at Wye to interview Mr and Mrs Post. They received, in due course, a very curious story.

The Posts said that in 1895 they agreed to foster a small child for a woman named Mrs Edwards, who was a nurse. When they took charge of the boy he was nine weeks old, and they did not think that he had been well cared for. Mrs Edwards agreed to pay them 5 shillings (25p) a week for their trouble and departed.

For more than two years the Posts had cared for the child, receiving their money regularly in notes signed by "Mrs Edwards" or "Nurse Elizabeth". Not surprisingly, the couple became attached to the boy, as did their niece and neighbour, Miss Sarah Urben.

Like a bolt from the blue came a letter from Mrs Edwards, announcing that she would be coming to take the child away from their care on 8th September 1897. The Posts were deeply upset, the more so since the infant had known no other parents, but Mrs Edwards duly arrived and was evidently determined to remove the boy.

Mrs Edwards stayed with the Posts for two nights, during which time she visited Ashford and purchased a large tin box and two padlocks. She showed these to the Posts, remarking that she had bought the box because it was cheap and that two padlocks were more secure.

The Posts were not interested in boxes or locks. They and their niece sought to persuade Mrs Edwards not to take the child, especially because he had whooping cough at the time.

The nurse would not be persuaded. She insisted that her son would enjoy the company of her brother's children, though the Posts feared that he would infect other children with whooping cough.

On 10th September the unlucky child was dressed smartly in a sailor suit with straw hat, ready to go with the mother he did not remember. Mrs Edwards said that she would take only one change of clothing for him and send for the rest. Tearfully the Posts and their niece asked if they might cut a lock of the little lad's hair. This was permitted, the bundle of clothes was put in the tin box, and mother and child left.

At Towcester Station (where they must have changed trains) the Stationmaster remembered the lady because of some perceived peculiarity of manner. He showed them to an empty Second Class carriage, collected an excess fare from her, and later recalled that she pulled down the blinds as soon as she had boarded the train. William Hooten was to recall that the blinds were still down when the train reached Ettington and the nurse, the bundle and the box emerged without the boy.

Questioned by the police, Elizabeth Brandish admitted that she was "Mrs Edwards". The boy was her illegitimate son, born when she had been nursing at Ashford, and bore the resounding names of Rees Thomas Yells Brandish. She claimed that while walking on the Clent Hills she had met a woman who wanted a child. Miss Brandish had offered to supply her with one, provided that no money changed hands and the woman never made any enquiry as to the boy's parentage. In pursuit of this arrangement she had retrieved her child from the Posts and met the woman on the train where the transfer was effected. She had expected to meet the woman in Birmingham a few days later and had gone there, but the woman had not appeared. She was unable to give the woman's name or address.

Elizabeth Brandish was held at Stratford upon Avon Police Station while the police considered the position. They did not believe the nurse's story, who could blame them, but difficulties threatened in the absence of a body. Common sense argued that the child had died on the train and been transported in the tin box, in which case he was most probably concealed somewhere about Drybank Farm, but it took them nine weeks to arrive at this conclusion, after searching every ditch, hedge, coppice and pool for miles.

Eventually four policemen descended on poor brother George's farm, with orders to dig up 60 square yards of his garden. They had nearly finished when Sergeant Smith of Shipston on Stour spotted something. Gardening used to be a popular hobby among rural policemen, perhaps it still is. We do not know if the Sergeant was a horticulturalist, but what he noticed was an anomaly. There were two rows of cabbages under the farmhouse windows and round the middle ones were traces of white powder. Sergeant Smith wondered why a gardener would spread lime only on the middle few and not on all the plants.

Quickly they dug into the cabbage patch and there they found the naked and doubled over body of a small child, surrounded by lime and badly decomposed.

An inquest opened at the Chequers Inn, drawing such a large audience that the room's partition wall had to be removed. It was soon adjourned to await scientific examination of the body. When the inquest reconvened, Miss Urben deposed that Rees Brandish had had 16 teeth, the top two rather wide. She produced her souvenir lock of hair which seemed to match that of the dead child. The identification was accepted.

The scientists who had examined the remains had been disadvantaged by the 9 weeks decomposition in lime, but seemed satisfied that the boy had not died of poison. Dr Fenton of Kineton thought the child had congestion of the throat and chest which had occurred twenty to forty minutes prior to death. He believed that Rees had been suffocated.

A verdict of wilful murder was returned against the mother and she was committed for trial at Warwick Assizes, where she appeared in March 1898. Lord Chief Justice Lord Russell of Killowen presided in a court packed with spectators.

George Brandish said that he knew nothing of a child of his sister's and admitted that there was so much lime kept about his farm that 30 or 40 pounds might be taken and he would not notice. His wife Louisa said that Elizabeth had confided in her that she had an illegitimate child, though when asked whether it had been born alive she only replied, "Yes".

Miss Celia Smith lived opposite the house where Nurse Brandish had worked in Clent. She recalled a Saturday in the previous October when heavy smoke had poured from the chimney of that house and she had seen Elizabeth peep - ing from behind the curtains. Police had raked the ash tip and uncovered pearl buttons, similar to those on Rees' smart sailor suit. They were also similar to the buttons on many of the smart sailor suits worn by children at that period.

Carriers from Ettington and Clent gave evidence of having transported the box, sometimes heavy and sometimes light. The prosecution argued that having murdered the boy on the train, Nurse Brandish concealed the body in the box, making it heavy. During a night at her brother's home she had buried the body, making the box light when she returned to Clent. There she had burned the child's clothing while her employer was away.

Most of the Jury were ready to convict, but one stood out for an acquittal and a retrial was ordered. That began in July. By now Elizabeth was showing a prison pallor.

Mr Justice Darling presided and the same evidence was led, together with that of a Police Sergeant Narramore from Clent. He described how Nurse Brandish had cared for his wife until Mrs Narramore died, leaving him with two teenage daughters. He might, he admitted, have proposed to Miss Brandish if "things had not cropped up".

The defence relied on the circumstantial nature of the case, while the prosecutor scouted Elizabeth's story of the woman in the Clent Hills, pointing out that the case had received enormous publicity in the Midlands for months and that, if there was such a woman, she would have come forward by now.

This time the Jury was able to agree - on a verdict of not guilty. Elizabeth Brandish stepped from the dock with a smile on her pale face.

How the second jury arrived at this verdict we cannot know. Perhaps they believed that nurses do not kill, yet it seems beyond doubt that Elizabeth Brandish murdered her son. The murder of a helpless child, especially by its mother, evokes a particular revulsion. What can have been her motive?

Sergeant Narramore was her motive. In Kent she had been betrayed and abandoned by a man. She was in her mid thirties, a single woman forced to work for a pittance and to depend upon her brother for any kind of a home. The prospect of marriage to a police sergeant with steady employment and a pension at the end must have exerted a very strong allure. There was only one fly in the ointment, Rees Thomas Yells Brandish. Police forces still exert far more influence over the private lives of their officers than any other employer; a century ago the moral code was even more strict. Sergeant Narramore would not, could not, have married a woman with an illegitimate child. So the boy had to be disposed of.

Elizabeth Brandish went back to nursing, soothing the sick with hands that had stifled her own little boy. The Posts and Miss Urben had two locks of hair to remind them of a loved child. Sergeant Narramore went sadly back to Clent.

The victim of this dreadful story was buried by the Parish Overseers of Ettington. The vicar was away, the only other clergyman, a Congregationalist, would not do it. So the child's coffin was buried with only two local women, the undertaker and his son standing by, no prayer, no service. Ettington Church is now a ruin, and Rees Thomas Yells Brandish lies in an unmarked grave somewhere under the lawns.

A recent account of the case states that no one has ever known who was the child's father. I would have thought that resoundingly strange name might be a clue and that a search among 1890s directories and registers of the residents of Ashford, Kent, might reveal his ancestry. Whatever his parentage, he deserved better than to be murdered by a mother crazed by the desire for her own security, and to end up buried like a stray dog.

Having Incautiously Repaired
(Erdington, Warks 1817)

Our pagan ancestors believed that the coming of summer was an important event and welcomed it on 1st May with ceremonies involving virgins and sacrifices. This date is our oldest public holiday. Christmas, Easter and Whitsun are Christian palimpsest, imposed upon older festivals, and August Bank Holiday is a 19th century creation.

The Church frowned on this celebration of summer. Kipling wrote that you must not let the parson know that you had "been out in the woods all night, conjuring summer in".

Gradually the church won, the wanton pleasures of May Day began to be absorbed into meaningless festivities, often moved to Whitsun. Well into this century, Wolverhampton used to stage a Whitsun parade of schoolgirls in white dresses, a pale echo of May Day.

In 1817 industrial towns were young and had not sprawled across miles of the landscape. Suburbs had not been invented and woods and fields reached right to the edges of the reeking factory towns.

The Tyburn House was a big, square pub at the junction of the Kingsbury Road and Chester Road. It has been replaced by a modern building of the same name and function on a main road corner amidst howling traffic, close to factories and the Castlevale Estate. In 1817 it was some miles from the bustle of Birmingham, in green fields, farms and woods, and there on 26th May 1817, was a Whitsun Dance.

Mary Ashford lived at Langley, near Sutton Coldfield and decided to go to the dance with her friend Hannah Cox. She took her dancing finery to Hannah's home at Erdington, intending to finish her business at Birmingham market early, change at Hannah's and go dancing. At about 6 o'clock she came and changed into her best clothes, a clean dress, white spencer (a kind of over jacket) and white stockings. In her low cut dress with her hair in the fashionable ringlets, she made a pretty picture as they set out for the ball.

It was no prince charming whose attention Mary caught at the Tyburn House, but a young man called Abraham Thornton from Castle Bromwich. He was a 25 year old bricklayer, stocky and thick necked. His eye having fallen on Mary, he asked a bystander who she was. Told that she was Mary Ashford, he is said to have replied, "I have had her sister, and I shall have her too".

Thornton and Mary danced together and, late at night, left the inn in company with another young couple. Hannah Cox went virtuously home to her single bed, believing (she said) that Mary had gone to her grandfather's. Mary and Thornton soon separated from their companions and wandered into the countryside. It was late May and the woods and meadows would have been at their best and, as Kipling observed, it was a common custom to be out in the woods all night, whether "conjuring summer in" or not.

At about 4.40 next morning, Hannah said, she was awakened by Mary knocking her door. She let her in, Mary changed into working clothes and left shortly before 5 o'clock.

A contempory engraving of Mary Ashford.

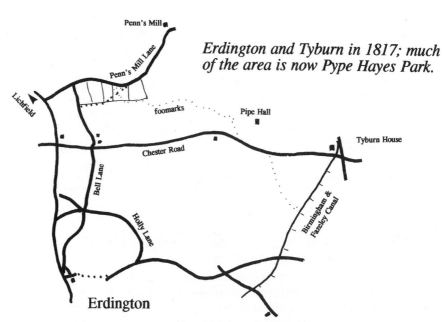

Erdington and Tyburn in 1817; much of the area is now Pype Hayes Park.

Holly Lane and Chester Road are still there. Penn's Mill Lane is now Penns Lane, Bell Lane is probably Orphanage Road and Pipe Hall now Pype Hayes Hall. Mary Ashford may be commemorated in the modern Ashford Drive near the Hall. The murder scene was in the area of modern Berwood Road.

On the same morning George Jackson was walking through the meadows on his way to work. He had just heard the church clock strike 5 o'clock when he came to a pool in a field of clover. There he noticed a bonnet and pair of shoes at the edge of the water filled gravel pit. Seeing that one shoe was bloodstained, Jackson went in search of help, and about two hours later the drowned corpse of Mary Ashford was dragged from the water.

Careful examination of the area revealed footprints and other marks in the soil and dew laden grass, and a diagram was drawn. It appeared that Mary and a heavier person had been involved in a chase across a harrowed field and along the edge of the clover meadow. Forty yards from the pit, grass was flattened in a human shape with arms outstretched and legs apart. Between the leg marks were the impressions of knees and a quantity of blood. Alongside the pit was a single, clear print of a man's shoe with two prominent nails.

At the nearby house of William and Fanny Lavell the body was examined. The dress was so blood stained that the lower area had to be ripped away, to reveal that the body was covered in blood around the legs. The arms were bruised as though she had been fiercely held. Two surgeons examined her, determining that she had been a virgin before a violent act of sexual intercourse, and that she carried no injuries except the bruises and those caused by the penetration.

It took little time to determine that she had left the Tyburn House with Abraham Thornton, and the landlord agreed to seek out the bricklayer. He found him at home, unaware of the discovery of Mary's body. Thornton said that he had been with her until about 4.00 in the morning and readily agreed to return to the Tyburn House.

At the inn, Thornton ate and chatted unconcernedly until the constable arrived, when he answered questions confidently. Basically he stated that he had had sex with Mary, but by her consent. He denied rape and knew nothing of her death.

Suicide had to be considered. Having given herself to Thornton, shame and remorse might have led her to do away with herself (it still, occasionally, does and was more common then), but it was thought unlikely.

Thornton was arrested and charged with rape and murder. He was tried at Warwick Assizes on 8th August in a courthouse outside which a mob was fighting with the court's javelin men for admission.

Evidence revealed that many people had seen Mary and Thornton, Mary alone, or Thornton alone during that short summer night, but timing was impossible. Watches were non existent among the labouring class and times were guessed by reference to earlier events and unreliable church clocks. This was a period when the only source of reference to set a clock was another clock and errors abounded. Each town and village maintained its own "time zone" by reference to its church or Town Hall clock.

The Defence argued that Hannah Cox's clock had been forty minutes fast, not an unlikely error in those days, and that it had been just about 4.00 am when Mary arrived. It was at least ten minutes from Hannah's home to the flooded gravel pit and they had a witness who had seen Thornton 3 miles distant at 4 o'clock.

Grave suspicion might cling to Thornton, but sufficient facts to hang him there were not. The Jury acquitted him on both counts and there the matter would normally have ended. However, Mary's most immediate kin was her 17 year old brother and some stupid or unscrupulous lawyer advised the boy that there was an ancient process known as an "Appeal of Murder" whereby he might have Thornton tried again. William Ashford commenced proceedings, Thornton was arrested in October and held in Warwick Gaol and the case moved into a new and bizarre phase.

An Appeal of Murder was not a criminal process to retry the case at assize or quarter session, but an action which took the case into the civil court of King's Bench. It was a survivor from Norman times, very rare and only available to the victim's nearest relative.

The case came on in London in November. Thornton was asked how he responded and astonished the Court by, quite literally, flinging down a gauntlet. How one would love to have seen the faces of the Judges, before whom and their predecessors no such act had taken place for almost two hundred years. In those two, long centuries His Majesty's Judges had forgotten the significance of the gesture, and it had to be explained to them by Thornton's Counsel that an Appeal of Murder was not the only forgotten process that could be revived. Thornton's symbolic act was a demand to be tried by battle, a typically Norman process unused since 1632.

Ashford's lawyers argued, hypocritically, that trial by battle was no longer available. It had been a barbarous process, they advised, whereby Ashford and Thornton would have been required to meet in single combat from sunrise to sunset or the death of one party. Against the robust and healthy bricklayer, their semi invalid teenage client stood no chance.

The legal arguments occupied many months. At one point Ashford's Counsel passionately declared that it would be an outrage if the law allowed Thornton, having murdered the sister, to go on to murder the brother.

"You must not", rebuked one of the Judges, "say murder, for if this Court were to decide that Trial by Combat is available, then it would be no murder".

That is exactly what they did decide, establishing the principle that a law is not dead because it has been forgotten; it must be specifically repealed by Parliament. Young Ashford did not, it seems, fancy his chances against Thornton and withdrew his proceedings.

Whether innocent or guilty, Thornton had had enough. The long drawn out case had killed his father and the public still believed him guilty. After an attempt by a Liverpool prostitute to publish a forged confession, he sailed for America.

Was he guilty? Well, he admitted having sex with Mary. Whether by rape or with her consent, it might have led to suicide. Suicides do commit strange acts like taking off their hats and shoes before dying. It may even have been an accident. Mary's body and dress were heavily bloodstained. Did she take off her hat and shoes and wade into the pool to cleanse herself and her clothing? It was big enough and deep enough to cause some trouble in recovering her body. Maybe Abraham Thornton was guilty as charged, but maybe he was guilty of rape and not of murder, or perhaps innocent of both.

In Warwick the graceful 18th century building where he was tried is still a court house and you can see the strange octagonal courtroom where Thornton was acquitted. Beneath it lies an octagonal dungeon with eight sets of irons attached to each corner. In brisker days, eight felons were held there, then fed rapidly up the central staircase to the dock so as not to slow down the wheels of justice.

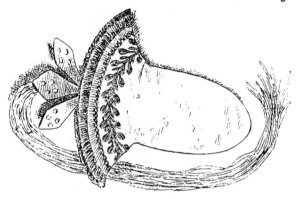

A bonnet, a fly whisk, or what? No, its the gauntlet.

Mary Ashford lies in Holy Trinity churchyard at Sutton Coldfield, her monument bearing a patronising inscription that has outraged many. Composed by a local cleric it says, in part:

"As a warning to female virtue and a humble monument to female chastity this stone marks the grave of MARY ASHFORD who in the 20th year of her age having incautiously repaired to a scene of amusement without proper protection was brutally violated and murdered on 27th May 1817."

Perhaps because she was ill used in life and denied justice in death, it is said that her ghost still runs through Erdington and knocks at Hannah Cox's door.

On Whit Monday of 1974, 157 years after Mary's death, a 20 year old Erdington Nurse, Barbara Forrest, visited a friend's home to change into a new dress and then went to a dance. Sometime early the next morning - 27th May, the precise anniversary of Mary's death, Barbara was raped and strangled. Her body was found less than 500 yards from the site of Mary's death. A man was arrested, his name was Thornton. In March 1975 Mr Justice Croom Johnson ruled that the evidence against him was insufficient and let him go free.

I Have Had Mine, Now..

(Dudley, Worcs 1855)

Many who know and admire the works of Charles Dickens
forget that his superbly drawn characters sprang not just
from a highly inventive imagination, but also from his long
experience as a journalist.

In 1855 Dickens was editing a magazine called *Household
Words*. It carried no news but ran a monthly supplement
known as the *Household Narrative*, a slender publication
crammed with small print which set out the doings of Parliament and the Courts, the activities of the Army and Navy,
Empire and foreign affairs, municipal actions, disasters
and crimes, as well as a Stock Exchange report, obituaries
of the famous and book reviews - all in about two dozen
pages. Here and there one can detect the hand and eye of
the Editor, where some of his enthusiasms loom large in
the narrow columns.

One cannot be sure if he saw everything that appeared in
print, but it is safe to guess that he read all the crime news.
The issue for May 1855 carried rather less criminal news
than usual, but the third item announced that "A dreadful
Murder was perpetrated at the village of Kate's Hill, near
Dudley, on Saturday morning, the 12th inst."

Seventeen year old Mary Ann Mason was a kitchen servant
at the Sailor's Return public house in Kates Hill. She lived
nearby in Woodside and had worked at the pub for only
seven weeks. Her father, a lay preacher, was concerned
for his daughter among the customers of a public house,
and demanded of William Hunt, the landlord, that he
keep an eye on Mary and ward off any young men.

It seems that her father was too late, for she already had a
follower in Joseph Meadows, a 23 year old apprentice gal-
vaniser at Dudley. Because of her father's prohibition, she
introduced Meadows at the Sailor's Return as her brother,
though some must have become suspicious of the time he
spent hanging about the inn's kitchen to talk to her.

For whatever reason (and it seems there was none) Meadows became convinced that Mary Ann's affections were wandering. Maybe he asked for what she was not prepared to allow him, and like many before and since, believed that her refusal was evidence that she did not love him. He became so convinced of her faithlessness that he resented it when she broke off their courting in the kitchen to serve drinks.

By early May he had decided that, if she was not his, no one else would have her. At his Round Oak home on the night of 11th May he did not go to bed, but fretted all night in a chair, finally deciding to kill Mary Ann.

Early next morning he left home, taking with him a carbine, powder and shot, belonging to his employer, Mr Rann, who was a member of the Dudley Troop of Yeoman cavalry.

Meadows arrived at the Sailor's Return between 6.00 and 7.00 am where the landlord served him a pint of ale. He took the drink to the kitchen and talked to Mary Ann while she scrubbed the floor. For two hours they chatted and he can have given no sign of his intention.

At about 9.00 am William Ingram and a man called Robinson entered the pub. They took drinks and sat in the kitchen. Perhaps it was this simple routine that finally cracked Meadows, for suddenly he produced the carbine from behind him, pointed it at Mary Ann and fired. The slugs struck her in the neck, the mouth and the left ear and she was dead in less than fifteen minutes. William Ingram said later,

> "I wondered what had happened. The report knocked my cap off. I ran to the prisoner and said to him: "You have murdered her. What did you do it for?""

Meadows made no answer until the Police arrived, when he told Superintendent Jewkes,

> "I have had my revenge, which they tell me is sweet. I have had mine, now the law must take its own".

Meadows was arrested and an inquest convened the same afternoon at the Sailor's Return, where Mary Ann's blood still stained the kitchen floor. A large crowd lined the route from Dudley to Kates Hill, striving to see the murderer as he passed, and when they saw him, howling "Hang him!".

Superintendent Jewkes described how he had examined the weapon and searched Meadows, then:

"One of the witnesses (William Hunt) had shouted "Oh you vagabond - you have shot your own sister" but Meadows whispered to me, on the way to the Station "It's not my sister. It's a young woman I've followed upwards of ten months and why I did it I shall never tell no-one"."

Dr Meredith deposed that, when he had arrived, Mary Ann was bleeding heavily from a gunshot wound in the neck. She had other wounds about the face and had died a few minutes after his arrival.

The miners Ingram and Robinson testified, as did Mr Rann, who said that the weapon was his and had been taken without his permission. Quickly the inquest found a verdict of wilful murder against Joseph Meadows. He was taken to Worcester Gaol where, perhaps as a mark of opinion, he was lodged in the condemned cell.

He took his trial at Worcester Assizes on 17th July 1855 before Chief Baron Pollok. The proceedings lasted less than a day and the jury spent only five minutes in returning a guilty verdict.

From the condemned cell he wrote (or signed with his mark what had been written for him) a letter to Mary Ann's parents:

"I know I have committed the most dreadful crime that man can be guilty of against God and you all and specially against one who was a most kind and affectionate sister to you all.

I believe it has caused many an aching heart but I hope and trust that it will be a caution to those given to lead a wicked and rebellious life like I did unto that time. Had I not led that life it would never have happened. Not that I upbraid any of you for it - it is merely to show you all what drinking brings on you."

It is known that Joseph Meadows could not write, and it is likely that the words and sentiments are those of the Prison Chaplain.

Shortly before 8.00 am on 28th July 1855 Meadows spoke his last words, to Executioner Calcroft of Dudley on the gallows in Worcester Gaol's yard. He said, "Do it quickly".

A postscript to the Kates Hill murder arose in 1991, after the *Black Country Bugle* had published the story. A lady wrote from Bournemouth to say that Joseph Rann, Meadows' master, was her great great grandmother's son, and she sent the *Bugle* a letter, ostensibly written to Mr Rann by Meadows from Worcester Gaol. It is even more of a religious tract than that quoted above. The *Bugle* were quick to spot the copper plate handwriting and the final "Yours Obediently, Joseph Meadows" and declare it a production of the Chaplain. Joe Meadows seems to have been a man of deeds, not words, and therein lay his and Mary Ann's fate.

Your Devoted Harry
(Stratford upon Avon, Warks 1954)

April 23rd means little to most people in England. A romantic few remember that it is Saint George's Day and raise their red cross banners or the union flag and wear a rose of England in their lapel. In Stratford upon Avon, however, it is a day of great importance. There the national Saint stands a long way behind the local hero in importance, for it is the birthday of Will Shakespeare. Do not debate there whether Bacon or someone else wrote those superb plays for you will be badly received. William Shakespeare has been the town's principal export and attraction for centuries and on his birthday the locals do their best to encourage and entertain the tourists who come on that special day.

Early on 24th April 1954 the sexton of Holy Trinity Church, Thomas Anderson, was making his way to the church along the Avon's banks when his eye caught a gleam in the grass. Stooping, he found a pair of gold rimmed spectacles. Nearby he found a set of lower dentures and a woman's shoe. When he reached the churchyard he saw that it showed signs of disturbance and, most astonishing of all, the footstone of a grave was missing.

Even a person who can tear an established tombstone from the ground will not carry it further than they have to, and Tom Anderson went quickly to the riverside to see if it had been thrown in. He did not see the missing stone, but he did see a brown felt hat. Now thoroughly alarmed he called the police.

The area was searched but no tombstone and no explanation was found. By 10.00 am the Police had decided to drag the river. The operation continued for more than six hours before they found a body. It was the corpse of a 45 year old woman, Olive May Gardner Bennett, and near to it lay the missing footstone.

Dr Barrowcliff examined the body. The woman was fully dressed, her hands were tightly clasped in front of her and clearly visible on her throat were the marks of the fingers that had strangled her. The hyoid bone in the neck was fractured (clear evidence of strangulation) and there were grazes to her knees and forearm. A fractured rib appeared to have been caused when the tombstone struck the body. Dr Barrowcliff put the time of death at between 11.00 pm and midnight on the previous night.

Superintendent Spooner of Warwickshire CID took charge of the enquiry, but in those days provincial police forces were not so large as nowadays and did not have the resources or the expertise now available. Then it was usual, if a murder enquiry became complex, to call on Scotland Yard's assistance and, within days, Superintendent Spooner did so. Now two more strangers arrived in Stratford, Superintendent Capstick and his assistant, Detective Sergeant Bill Heddon.

With no obvious motive for the murder, the detectives began to reconstruct Olive Bennett's life, in the hope that something in it would give them a lead. They found that she had been born in Edinburgh in 1908. Her parents were both still living, John Fraser Bennett at 75 and his wife, Anne, at 69. There had been a younger daughter, but she had died at 18.

When Olive was 5 her family had moved to York. She had been quite well educated, spending some time at Edinburgh University at the age of 19. She had intended a career in teaching but could not achieve the necessary grades, so she tried social work. Her parents could not support her financially in this and she turned to nursing. In 1939 she qualified at Birmingham as a State Certified Midwife and in 1945 began her studies to become a State Registered Nurse, succeeding three years later, though she promptly returned to midwifery which she said she preferred.

Throughout this time she had been under a great deal of pressure from her mother, a grimly religious woman. Catherine McLeod, a cousin of Olive, told the detectives that there had been a romance with a airman during the War, but Mrs Bennett had discovered and put an end to it, telling Olive to concentrate on her career, not men.

On another occasion Mrs Bennett had found Olive writing a letter to a man called Reg. Rifling her daughter's handbag, which was apparently her custom, the mother found a cautious letter to Olive from "Reg" and stormed at her daughter. Olive said she had met Reg while on a course at Birmingham University and that he was something to do with farm machinery. She did not have his address, but wrote to him at a club in London. Mrs Bennett not only commanded Olive to break off the relationship, she wrote to Reg at his club, telling him to stay away from her daughter or she and her husband would "take steps".

The police, however, learned a different story from the one which Olive told her mother. Reg responded to press publicity and, despite being a married man with four children, contacted the Police and told them of his relationship with Olive.

They not met at Birmingham University but on a dark night in June 1953 at Worcester. Reg, a commercial traveller, was watching the fireworks with which the city celebrated Queen Elizabeth's Coronation. Near him in the gloom was a short, plain woman with glasses. As the last rockets burst and died above them, Reg turned away, saying aloud. "Well, that's it then. I'm off for a drink". He undoubtedly intended this as an invitation and, as such, it worked. The little woman responded by making it quite clear that she was available and their chance encounter turned into an affair. Olive was then working at Shrub Hill Hospital in Worcester and when Reg's work brought him to the Mid- lands, they met in various hotels. She was he said, sexually experienced but normal. Their last tryst had been in Reading, about a fortnight before her death.

It might be thought that Reg was wriggling his way out of a murder enquiry by blackening the reputation of the little midwife, but the Police believed him and eliminated him from their enquiries, for what he had told them, so far from being unusual, fitted very well with what they were learning about Olive Bennett.

In the same year that the Queen was crowned and Reg met Olive, something had disturbed her life deeply, so that her patterns of behaviour and her morals changed in a way that undoubtedly culminated in her murder. Evidence was accumulating which showed that, while working at Shrub Hill, Olive Bennett had developed a habit of picking up men in Worcester. Along with an apparently insatiable appetite for sex, she acquired a taste for sherry and took to smoking heavily. She would drink sherry alone in the city's pubs, sometimes being thrown out by landlords. If she had not made a pick up in a pub, she would sometimes leave, then return in feigned agitation and say that she was afraid that she was being followed. If this did not call forth a volunteer, she was not above leaving again and repeating the performance. Often when she left a pub she would buy a bottle of sherry to take out.

In that Coronation summer she began to draw regularly on her savings account. Previously she had built it up in small increments, but from then on it was all withdrawals.

In 1954 she went to work at the Monroe Devis Maternity Home in Stratford upon Avon, and was soon as well known in Stratford's pubs as she had been in Worcester. This time her story was that she was afraid to cross Clopton Bridge alone at night and, again, she was quite prepared to give repeat performances. Servicemen from Long Marston Camp admitted they had known her and had sex with her, though · she had paid for their drinks.

As well as researching Olive's background, the Police also attempted to reconstruct her movements on the night of Will Shakespeare's birthday. They discovered that the idea of all those strangers in town made Olive anxious to get off duty and into town, so anxious she didn't even eat before going out.

They had sightings of her in the George Hotel and the Red Horse in the town centre, drinking sherry but alone. She was seen leaving the Red Horse at 10.30 pm, but the same witness saw her again, an hour later, still standing outside the hotel.

At 11.30 she stopped a night watchman who was going on duty. He thought she seemed angry, but she asked him how she could get a lift to Shipston on Stour, about 10 miles away. He suggested that she wait at the junction of Clopton Bridge and the Shipston Road. We do not know if she did.

What may be the last sight of her, except by the murderer, was by an hotel porter who saw a couple embracing in Holy Trinity churchyard. He thought that the woman might have been Olive, but he was unsure because he thought them a courting couple and paid little attention.

Several hundred statements were taken, from residents, visitors and transients, but no clues surfaced. The film from television cameras recording the festivities was pored over in the hope that it might reveal Olive and a companion, but without success. A Long Marston soldier was questioned more than once after a pair of Olive Bennett's knickers was found in his kit. His wife failed to confirm his story that she had given them to him to clean his equipment. He admitted knowing and having had sex with Olive and strenuous efforts were made to track his movements on the night of the murder, no easy task for he had been on a protracted and enthusiastic pub crawl which even he could not fully remember.

Even Capstick of the Yard - "Charlie Artful" to the press - was getting nowhere, but there was one remaining clue. In her room at the Monroe Devis Home the Police had found a postcard. It had been sent from Carmarthen in West Wales on 16th March 1954 to Olive at Worcester. It made two appointments, for Wednesday and Thursday at "the G.W", which detectives took to mean Worcester's Great Western Hotel which Olive frequented while working at Shrub Hill. The card was signed "Harry".

Considerable press publicity was given to this clue, but unlike Reg, Harry did not come forward. Nevertheless, the circulation of the name in connection with the murder produced a strange result.

Two and a half weeks after the murder, Mr Hector Gray, a bookmaker in a northern town, left his shop and went to mount his bicycle. He noticed that a fragment of paper had stuck to his front wheel and lodged under the mudguard. Pulling it out he saw that it was an incomplete letter which included references to "Stratford", "Harry" and "Miss B". He saw the possibility that this related to the widely reported murder and passed it at once to the Police. It said:

"and I was not going to let her get 20 quid out of a poor thing like you. You know you should have had the Baby out and above Board, shouldn't you dear, and now she is where she will never do any more Blackmailing for a long time. Just forget about Miss B and your unfortunate experience, the baby will be well cared for and you can have her at any time you wish, also you will be 20 quid better off. Just forget the whole ghastly business

Your devoted Harry

I am returning to Stratford tomorrow, Tues. By road, see you in a weeks time, will tell you how Baby is then, don't worry dear."

The letter is certainly about blackmail. Is it about illegal abortion by a Certified Midwife? Is it about an arrangement to deliver a child in secret? Was "Miss B" that midwife? Perhaps more to the point, was "devoted Harry" the man who sent Olive the Carmarthen postcard? Was there no one in Britain who could recognise the handwriting of Harry who used capital Bs when he should use small ones? Apparently not.

Capstick's team traced a dozen Harrys who had had slender connections with Olive, but questioned and eliminated them all. The enquiry slowed down, the men from Scotland Yard went home and, more than forty years later, Olive Bennett's murderer remains uncaught.

However, embedded in this sad story is another mystery. What turned the little, mother dominated midwife into a loose woman, endlessly seeking sex without even charging for it?

Early in 1952 she went to a doctor after suffering bouts of giddiness. Blood tests showed that she had cerebral syphilis, probably inherited. She was treated with injections at a Birmingham Venereal Disease Clinic, but the medical reports, although they said that her condition was not infectious and not communicable through sexual intercourse, also said that it was affecting her brain. Although she was "not exactly mentally deficient", there was an obvious threat of paresis of the insane, the frequent outcome of the disease. Poor Olive Bennett, a trained Nurse, must have realised what lay before her. Was her behaviour a wild protest against the mother who had infected her, and apparently knew it from the way she warned Olive away from men? Were the sherry and sex sessions defiant banners flown by a woman in her mid forties who had nothing to lose and nothing to look forward to except the wretched darkness of syphilitic insanity? One medical report suggested that her change of behaviour was itself a symptom of the deepening grip of her disease. Whatever the reason, it led her to her doom at Trinity Church, perhaps a better end than she might otherwise have known.

As to her killer, Superintendent Spooner believed it was a local man. A man because it would be a remarkable woman who could rip a 75 five year old tombstone from its setting, and local because Olive, a stranger to Stratford herself, usually took her men to parks and waste ground, not to the churchyard.

Was it Harry that she waited for inside and outside the Red Horse? Was she angry with him for not keeping an appointment? Did he live in Shipston on Stour? Did he turn up, late, to find her at the Clopton Bridge junction, or was she so angry with him that she picked up someone else who took her to Trinity churchyard? She was not robbed and she gave sex eagerly to strangers, so what led to her death?

From time to time as the years passed, press stories appeared about the questioning of a man in connection with Olive's death; on at least one occasion it was in Canada. None of them led anywhere. If Olive Bennett's killer was a young man, he could still be alive. If he was Olive's age, or older, he would be very old or dead. Olive lies in Alveston churchyard, two miles from Holy Trinity, Stratford on Avon. Perhaps her killer lies in another graveyard, or perhaps not.

As A Man Falleth
(Stone, Staffs 1781)

The Staffordshire Moorlands in sunny weather can show as pleasant a face as anywhere in England, but they stand so high above the rest of the county that they are frequently swept by rain and snow. Then they show a grimmer, more forbidding aspect.

The hamlet of Rushton Spencer lies below Biddulph Moor. To motorists on the main road it is gone in a blink. They might just catch a glimpse of the Church of Saint Lawrence the Martyr, perched high on a bluff to the west, with its graveyard clinging to the slope.

Turn up the lane beside the filling station, follow its windings onto the moor and you will come to the lonely little church, which has been called the "chapel in the wilderness". Its door still bears 17th century graffiti and gravestones of similar age cluster around it.

Walk round to the rear of the church. The graveyard has been extended in recent years but you will find a group of 18th century tombstones around a lowering yew tree. Among them are stones of the Meaykin family and one in particular may catch your eye because it is set at the wrong end of the grave. It is the grave of Thomas Meaykin and as well as its unusual setting, it has a bizarre and still legible inscription:

Memento Mori
Thomas, son of Thomas and Mary Meaykin.
Interred July 16th 1781 aged 21 years.
As a man falleth before wicked men, so fell I.
Bia Thanates.

A country tombstone for an unknown youth in three languages? "Remember Death" warns the first line in Latin; "Death by violence" declares the last line in Greek; but in between is no date of death and that strange quote about wicked men. The mossy stone has stood for more than two centuries as a reminder of a peculiarly hideous murder, uncovered by what seems to have been supernatural means.

Thomas Meaykin was a son of the village, as the family stones about his resting place testify, but he found employment as a groom and houseboy in the little Staffordshire town of Stone. He should have been successful, for animals liked him and so did people, but he attracted one person who made his life difficult.

His master had a young daughter who made overtures to the groom. There is no evidence that he ever responded to her advances or trespassed upon her willingness, quite the reverse. Keenly aware of his place, he rebuffed her, but her attempts to ensnare him and his avoidances became the subject of local gossip and amusement.

Her father was not amused. There was, in those days, an emerging class of educated men who were not yet accepted as professionals in the modern sense. They knew that they were not of the common people, but the aristocracy and the landed gentry treated all of them as tradesmen and looked down upon them. As a consequence, doctors, lawyers and apothecaries were unduly sensitive of their social position. No apothecary's daughter was going to marry a mere groom. Her place was to marry upwards. Her wretched father must have winced at the town's gossip and fretted to find a solution.

Suddenly fate seemed to take a cruel hand. Young Tom fell ill and despite his master's drugs, soon died. He was quickly buried, not where he now lies on Biddulph Moor, but in the churchyard of Saint Michael's at Stone, and there, but for a completely inexplicable event this sad little tale might have ended.

It was not only his many human friends who grieved for Tom, so did his favourite pony. Often it would find its way to his grave and paw restlessly at the earth that covered its master. This piteous performance went on so long that it crystallised the fears of those who thought the youth's death untimely and his burial hasty.

So it was that on a summer morning in 1782, they had Thomas Meaykin's grave opened. It is impossible to imagine their horror and dismay at what they found, for when the coffin was opened Thomas, who had been buried face upwards, was lying face down - he had been buried alive.

Now Stone gossiped again, but this time without amusement. Now there was talk of his master's vengeance and of a regime of drugs that an apothecary might use to put someone into a death like sleep. There was no prosecution because science was still uncertain and an educated apothecary would make a dangerous enemy.

Thomas's grieving family took him home to Rushton Spencer and there the unhappy lad was buried the wrong way round so that, according to the superstition of the day, his vengeful spirit could not rise and walk. It is hard to blame their fear; after all, by what agency had his terrible death been uncovered?

It was no superstitious countryman who wrote the inscription for Thomas's grave; it must have been a clergyman or schoolteacher to encapsulate Thomas Meaykin's frightful story in a trilingual epitaph that, despite the moorland wind and rain, still makes its accusation more than two hundred years later.

The second grave of Thomas Meaykin.

My Harem Takes Me

(Hardingstone, Northants 1930)

Every 5th November the English remember an attempted
murder. Guido (Guy) Fawkes and his co-conspirators were
betrayed as they tried to blow up Parliament for their religion. Centuries later they are remembered with bonfires
and fireworks. In November 1930 in the village of Hardingstone, Northamptonshire, a village dance had been moved
from Thursday night to Wednesday, so as to coincide with
the occasion.

At twilight the fires were lit and stuffed effigies of Guy
burned. By 1.45 am on Thursday, the children were fast
asleep and even the adults' dance was ended. So it was
that two young men, Alfred Brown and William Bailey,
were sauntering homewards.

As they turned into Hardingstone Lane they saw a bright
fire ahead of them. At the same time, a man who wore
no hat and carried an attache case emerged from a ditch.

"It looks as if someone has had a bonfire", he called to them sounding breathless. Reaching the junction, he turned first towards Northampton, then towards London, then paused in the middle of the road. He seemed to be watching them, but they took no further notice of him. They had seen that the fire ahead of them was roaring 15 feet into the air from around a small motor car. They ran into the village, where William Bailey alerted his father, the local Constable and he brought another officer, PC Copping.

By the time they returned to the car the flames were dying down. Soon they realised that there was a body in the vehicle and tried to douse the flames, but by the time this was done the car was totally gutted.

At 3.10 am Inspector Lawrence and PC Valentine arrived. Removal of the body and examination of the car began.

The corpse lay, face down, with its head in the driver's seat and its body across the passenger seat. The right arm might have been over the back of the passenger seat but had been burned off at the elbow. The left leg was bent up beneath the trunk and the extended right leg burned off. PC Copping later recalled that "the body did not quite look as if the person had been sitting in the passenger's seat and had fallen forwards into the driver's seat".

Where the nearside running board had been, the right leg extended about 8 inches from the car's chassis, the foot being burned off about 8 inches from the ankle. A charred boot heel was about 6 inches left of the running board, on the edge of the grass verge.

The corpse was wrapped in sacks and taken to the garage of the Crown Inn at Hardingstone. It was believed to be female and murder was not suspected.

The car, a Morris Minor carrying registration number MU 1468, was standing about a foot from the verge pointing towards the main road. It seemed to have stopped without vigorous braking.

PC Valentine opened the bonnet, removed the petrol filler pipe and examined the tank by torchlight. Strapped in front of the dashboard position, the petrol tank was empty and showed no rupture or leak. Behind the driver's seat was a petrol can which had burst. Its screw cap and handle were gone.

By 4.45 am it was necessary to clear Hardingstone Lane which, despite the name, was a tarmac road 18 feet wide carrying several bus routes. The car was shifted onto the verge and routine enquiries began.

Checking the registration revealed that the owner of the car was Alfred Arthur Rouse, of 14 Buxted Road, London N12. Metropolitan Police officers called on Mrs Rouse, who seemed to believe that her husband, a travelling salesman, had visited her at 1.00 am that day.

While Northamptonshire Police sought a missing woman, Dr Eric Shaw examined the body in the garage of the Crown Inn. Although the genitals and the chest wall were missing, he declared it to be the body of a grown man, about 5' 8" tall and in his early thirties.

The Police were still not seeking a murderer, though Inspector Lawrence later claimed that he was suspicious from the start, but the newspapers were developing a case. They found the hatless man with an attache case intriguing, as a man in an overcoat and no hat was more of a rarity then than a man in an overcoat with a hat is now.

Mrs Rouse could not confirm that the burned remains were those of her husband and the identity of the dead man was canvassed. Hundreds claimed him as a missing husband, son, father or friend. None could establish their claim and he remained unidentified. A description of Mr Rouse, said (wrongly) to be "a traveller for a firm dealing in women's costumes" was published. A newspaper containing it was delivered to a villa in Gellygaer, Monmouthshire, a Welsh reporter picked up a recollection from someone who had given a lift to Mr Rouse, and suddenly a seemingly accidental death became a murder.

Alfred Arthur Rouse was then 36 years old. He had been born in Kent, son of a hosier. From the age of 6 he was raised by his aunt. Educated at a council school, he worked in a soft goods store and became a sacristan at Saint Saviour's Church, Stoke Newington. He volunteered within days of the start of the Great War, becoming a private in the Queen's Territorial

Regiment. In the same year he married Lily May Watkins.

In 1915 he was seriously injured in the head, thigh and leg
near Festubert by fragments from an exploding shell. After
months in hospital he was discharged as unfit for service in
1916. We are told that there was little to his discredit at
that point in his life, although he fathered a son in France.

Whether the war injuries or experiences affected him I
do not know, but the discharged soldier changed. From a
hard working, church going young man he turned into what
Americans term a hustler. He changed jobs (always to his
betterment it must be said) and deployed his glib tongue
and good looks as a commercial traveller. On 5th November
1930 he was working for W B Martin & Co, dealers in men's
braces, garters and mackintoshes, earning about £500 a year.
He bought several cars in succession at a time when the
purchase of one car was beyond the dreams of most, and
became a skilled mechanic. Now he had reasons to travel,
the means to travel independently and the opportunity to
philander, which he exploited to the full. Shop assistants,
nurses, maids, all fell to his charm and lies. For of course
he did not tell them that he was a commercial traveller, a
discharged private soldier. He was always a Major in the
war, son of a lovely and distinguished mother (not the lady
who had deserted him at 6) who had sent him to Eton and
Cambridge. It was the stuff that many young girls dreamt
(and dream?) of and kept him well supplied with companions on his travels.

Fatherhood was not confined to that wartime instance in
France. In October 1921, Helen Campbell, a 15 year old
maid bore Rouse's child, but it died in a few weeks. He had
seduced Helen when she was 14. With the child dead Helen
returned to her employers where she met Rouse again, and
became pregnant once more. "Major" Rouse did the decent
thing, he married Helen in Islington in November 1924. The
happy couple moved into Liverpool Road, Islington, where
Rouse was a loving father to his son, born in July 1925.

Some months before the birth of his third(?) child, Rouse
had met Nellie Tucker, a servant girl in Hendon. She was
a lively 17 year old and soon became another of Alfred
Arthur's conquests. He offered marriage in cautious terms,
"when trade improves".

He was of course, already married to Lily, with whom in 1927, he moved to a house in Buxted Road, Finchley which he was purchasing for £50. He soon became popular in the locality, though not with men who found this glib, boastful, non smoking, non drinking man poor company.

In 1928 Nellie Tucker, who had borne Rouse a daughter, obtained a maintenance order against him. The child was fostered at 12/6d (62.5) per week, but Rouse's payments were sporadic.

Meanwhile disruption threatened his happy home in Islington. Helen Campbell had maintained herself by work in restaurants, but she and Rouse fell out over her taking one particular job. They separated, Helen keeping their son, but Rouse was less than a good provider and Helen too obtained a maintenance order in October 1929. Once again, his payments were irregular.

Somehow a meeting was held between the Rouses and Helen Campbell and an arrangement made that the little boy should be taken into Lily's home. In so far as Lily Rouse treated the child well, it worked.

A week before the Hardingstone Lane bonfire, on 29th October 1930, Nellie Tucker gave birth to another girl baby by Rouse. He visited her on the eve of the murder, depressed, anxious and watching the clock all the time. He mentioned the possibility of him losing his job and grew annoyed when she told him how soon she would leave hers. His unease made her ask, "Are you meeting any one?". "No", he replied, then admitted that his financial obligations were so heavy he didn't know where to turn. Telling her he must go north on business, he left at 8 o'clock.

If he had told Nellie many lies, he spoke the truth about his finances. His income was in the region of £10 per week, but his outgoings were rapidly overtaking it: £1/12s (£1.60p) a week on his car, £1/7/6d (£1.37.5) on the mortgage, at least £2 per week housekeeping to his wife, plus at least two maintenance orders. He had more women, perhaps, than has ever been revealed. Apart from Lily, Helen and Nellie, there was certainly one in Southampton, another in Birmingham and more elsewhere. As well as the children noted above, there was at least one other child in England.

There were other difficulties. His persistent bragging to his colleagues and acquaintances about his sexual conquests exposed Rouse to blackmail. One of his "wives" believed that it had happened. In addition, Lily knew of Helen and Nellie and was already contemplating leaving him when she found Ivy Jenkins' photo in his pocket.

Ivy Jenkins was both similar to and different from his other partners. The daughter of a colliery owner at Gellygaer, Monmouthshire, she was not a friendless working class girl, but she and her family were fooled by Rouse. He told them that he and Ivy were married, that he had just paid £125 on a lovely house in Kingston for her with beautiful furnishings. On 5th November 1930 Ivy Jenkins was pregnant and very ill, but her "husband" had promised to call the next day and take her home.

The foregoing account of Rouse's troubles may give a slight, but only slight, impression of the mood of desperation in which he left Nellie on Guy Fawkes's Night. As he told her, he was going to drive north, but on what business? We already know that somewhere on his way he acquired a passenger, that he stopped in Hardingstone Lane, that his car caught fire and his passenger died, while Alfred Arthur Rouse slipped away with his attache case - and no hat.

What he might have done had he not been seen by Brown and Bailey in Hardingstone Lane is pure speculation. Perhaps he intended to disappear completely or to establish his identity as Ivy Jenkins' husband. It seems that he had been offered the opportunity to become financially involved in a useful scheme in South Wales, and he could have believed that Gellygaer was a safe refuge.

Even if that was his plan, with his picture all over the national press it had to change. We are told that he went home to Buxted Road, arriving about 1.00 am according to his wife. That was impossible and it seems more likely that it was around 6.00 am and Lily Rouse, wakening suddenly in the dark, was confused. Rouse later said that the visit was "to tell my wife not to be worried"; worried at his disappearance, presumably, since he did not then know that the press would soon be hunting him. Did he change clothes while at home? We do not know. When the Police called it was to ask Lily to identify the remains from the car, not to catch a murderer, and the house was never searched.

He had reached London by hitching a lift in a lorry. From Buxted Road he made for Gellygaer by coach, and there he was forced to change his plans. The *Daily Sketch* of 7th November carried a story about his car, himself and, worst of all, his wife. He could not now face the Jenkins family.

Doubling back, he set out for London by coach. His habit of boasting and chattering trapped him. On the way down to Gellygaer he had talked to the coach driver, including remarks about his car. The driver spoke to a journalist friend who told the police. As Rouse's charabanc reached London at 9.20 pm on 7th November, it was stopped on Hammersmith Bridge by two detectives and Rouse was invited to a police station.

Questioned at Hammersmith Police Station, he said that he had picked up an apparently respectable hitch hiker bound for the Midlands. Later he lost his way and was spoken to by a policeman about his lights. Rouse became suspicious of his passenger, believing that the man was trying to steal his case. He was growing sleepy and the engine started to spit as though low on petrol. He pulled into Hardingstone Lane to relieve himself and asked the passenger to fill the tank from an extra can in the car. The passenger asked him for a cigarette, but Rouse refused. Rouse was some distance along the lane and had just pulled his trousers up when the Morris burst into flames. He had rushed back, seen the passenger in the car, but could not rescue him because it was a mass of flames. Panicking and feeling responsible for the accident, he ran away and saw two men. Having lost his head completely, he could not really account for his actions since.

He was asked if he had rescued his attache case from the car, and said that he had it with him when he got out because of his suspicions of the hitch hiker.

At 1.00 am Northampton officers arrived in London, Superintendent Brumby and Inspector Lawrence. They took a written statement from Rouse, substantially the same as his account to the Metropolitan detectives. The fire he could not explain; his actions afterwards were due to panic. It might have been true.

Taken to Angel Lane Police Station, Northampton, he was
told at noon told that the Inquest on the hitch hiker was
to be that afternoon. He enquired if Lily would be there
and could he see her. "Later", said Inspector Lawrence,
but again Rouse's mouth ran on:

> "She is already too good for me. I like a woman who will
> make a fuss of me. I don't ever remember my wife sitting
> on my knee, but otherwise she is a very good wife. I am
> friendly with several women, but it is a very expensive
> game ..... My harem takes me several places and I am
> not at home a great deal, but my wife doesn't ask
> questions now."

A little later he and Lily met. He wept, embraced her, told
her not to worry and to sell their home for defence funds,
then asked the Superintendent if she could have the 6/3d
(31.5p) which was all he had. He promptly asked Lily to buy
him some books and an ounce of John Cotton tobacco, leaving
her only the fare to London and the opportunity to walk from
the terminus to Barnet.

The committal proceedings on a charge of murder were heard
before the Northampton County Magistrates over five days in
November and December. D L Finnemore, a Birmingham
barrister, defended Rouse. Evidence was given of his life-
style and Inspector Lawrence deposed to the harem remarks.

The function of committing Magistrates is merely to decide
whether, on the evidence before them, a charge seems to be
founded and the defendant should stand trial. They establish
whether there is a prima facie case but do not decide guilt.
In those days all major crimes were subject to the process.
Now committal proceedings are often conducted by delivery
of written statements to the Court, or completely evaded
by the Crown Prosecution Service certifying that the matter
is suitable for trial in a Crown Court. In the few instances
where witnesses are called, modern magistrates tend to
commit for trial without proper consideration of the issues,
depriving a wrongly accused person of a valuable safeguard
and sometimes prejudicing the higher court. One Judge told
a lawyers' conference a few years ago, "once someone has
been committed you can be pretty sure that he is guilty".

That was not, however, Alfred Arthur's predicament. Evidence may be put before the magistrates which would be inadmissible at the trial, such as the highly prejudicial account of Rouse's affairs and his even more damning harem remarks. They were not necessary to build a prima facie case against him, but in two strokes the police had prejudiced both the magistrates and, what was far more important, the future jury. In those days there was no ban on reporting committal evidence, and the harem comment was widely and emphatically reported.

Evidence was also led to show that Rouse's car insurance gave a benefit of £1,000 in the event of the death of Rouse or a passenger while Rouse was driving. In fact this type of benefit had been a routine, free extra feature of motor insurances from almost the time they started, and still is. To refer to it in court was a mischievous attempt to lend the benefit a significance it did not possess. In any event, the prosecutor never has to establish a motive for a crime and one wonders how a vanished Rouse, believed dead, could have claimed against the policy.

Not surprisingly he was committed for trial, which began at County Hall, Northampton on 16th January 1931. Public interest was enormous because of the still unknown victim and the possibility of scandalous disclosures.

Mr Justice Talbot presided, Mr Finnemore led the defence and Mr Norman Birkett, an "advocates' advocate" - led the prosecution.

In his opening speech, Birkett pointed out that failure to identify the victim did not matter. He would prove that Rouse had murdered his passenger by setting fire to the car, probably after stunning the victim with a mallet. As to motive, the crown did not have to put forward a motive and it would not do so. At last someone had realised the difficulty over the insurance, but the jury might think that Rouse had intended the body to be taken for his, said Birkett. After the arguments about dubious evidence in the committal, the crown had stripped its case down to a deadly minimum.

After preliminary evidence in which Northamptonshire Police officers disagreed with each other about the position of the body and the time at which the car was moved, Inspector

Lawrence testified to taking Rouse' statement, offering the opinion that the Defendant had been lying.

Then came the technical evidence, a motor engineer to state that the Morris had been left in second gear, followed by Colonel Cuthbert Buckle, full pay Colonel commanding a Territorial brigade, Companion of the Order of the British Empire, Companion of the Noble Order of the Bath and twenty six years a fire assessor.

The fire had been extraordinarily intense in his view. He had never before seen a lower radiator water joint burn out in a car fire. The brass windscreen surround was cut through at bottom and top, and brass fuses at 1850 degrees. There had been, he said, an unusually intense fire under the bonnet which had been fed for some time.

Immediately below the cuts in the windscreen frame he examined the nut of the tap on the main fuel line. It was one whole turn loose. He had experimented on a police car with the same system, and found that slackening the nut by three quarters of a turn gave a free flow of petrol. He had filled a half pint tumbler in 80 seconds. That the nut came loose by accident he found hard to believe, suggesting that a lot of drivers would have died if that were so.

The idea of a bursting carburettor causing the fire he scouted, admitting that the carburettor had burst at some point. Throughout cross examination he returned again and again to his view of an intense fire. If leaking petrol had fired from a carelessly handled match, he believed it would have been a less fierce fire and easy to escape from.

When he left the witness box, the Colonel told Birkett that he had watched Rouse react to his evidence. The defendant kept tensing one knee when a certain part of the car was mentioned, then relaxing when Buckle did not say what Rouse seemed to fear.

Medical evidence followed and Dr Shaw revealed that, in a second post mortem he had found something strange. Between the left knee and the body was unburnt clothing - still moist with petrol. In other words, Colonel Buckle's 1,850 degree blaze had never reached near enough to even evaporate the petrol on that cloth, so that the defence argument that the knee had been contracted into that position by the heat could not be true. He also examined a mallet found near the car. There was neither blood nor skin upon it, but a few hairs of a lightish colour which might have been human.

Sir Bernard Spilsbury, eminent pathologist, added weight to the crown's case. The passenger, he said, had died within half a minute of the fire starting. The body position was not consistent with someone trying to get out, but with the deceased having been dropped or fallen face down. The position of the legs suggested that the door had been open. As to the petrol soaked cloth, it must either have become soaked very early in the fire or been soaked before the fire started.

There followed a long succession of witnesses giving brief evidence: young ladies whose carefully edited stories deeply disappointed the public gallery, witnesses from South Wales, a ticket seller, a coach driver, a fellow camper who identified the mallet as Rouse's and the embarrassed Superintendent Brumby. In the light of Rouse' claim to have left the car to answer a call of nature, a search had been made of the lane. The Superintendent could not find a euphemism for the object of the search, finally adopting a roundabout expression - "I mean that I went to look for what would have come from him". He did not find it and at that point the crown closed its case.

Alfred Arthur Rouse entered the witness box and gave substantially the same story he had told the Police. After the accident he had told lies in Wales because there were ladies present. He did not know what had happened in the car immediately before the fire, but he had done nothing wrong in Hardingstone Lane.

Norman Birkett, a cunning cross examiner, began to take Rouse through his lies, through his opportunities to come clean about the "accident" and through his mechanical expertise. Pressing Rouse to hold the exhibited carburettor in his hand, Birkett challenged him with having removed the top of the carburettor so that he could ignite it from the roadside and let it set the leaking petrol union alight. In his rambling fashion, Rouse stuck to his story. Birkett proved that the car's tank could not have needed topping up in Hardingstone Lane and, finally, that the flames must have roared 15 feet high for 6 to 8 minutes after the fire began.

As Rouse returned to the dock he said, "Only three Sundays left for me, I suppose", referring to the three clear Sundays expected to pass before an execution.

The jury took an hour and a quarter to return a guilty verdict. Colonel Buckle must have congratulated himself on spotting Rouse's reaction when the carburettor was mentioned.

An appeal was turned down; the Attorney General refused leave to appeal to the House of Lords; the Home Secretary refused a reprieve. The execution was set for 10th March. On the 9th the *News of the World* said Rouse had confessed. Next day the *Daily Express* quoted Mrs Rouse's denial.

On the morning of 10th March Alfred Arthur Rouse, swaying on his feet, was led to execution. On the morning of 11th March the *Daily Sketch* published his confession.

His motive had been his financial difficulties. He had made the acquaintance of an unemployed man at the Swan and Pyramid pub in Whetstone, and had offered him a lift to Leicester on Bonfire Night to look for work. He had supplied his passenger with whiskey, so that he was drunk by the stop in Hardingstone Lane. There Rouse had strangled him senseless or dead, loosened the fuel union, opened the carburettor, laid a 10 yard trail of petrol to the car and lit it. He had intended to put his Army identity disc on the dead man, but forgot.

Rouse passed briefly into folklore. Eddie Cantor's "Making Whoopee" was re-written by street balladeers:

> There was a man, his name was Rouse,
> He had the key to every house,
> He was suspected and then arrested
> For making whoopee!

Nobody, even Rouse, remembered the victim. In his confession Rouse said that he thought the man was a southerner, but he knew nothing about him. He was mentioned last at the trial as an incomplete corpse preserved in a tank. He has never been identified.

This Unfortunate Woman
(Rugeley, Staffs 1839)

Colin Dexter's Inspector Morse novels, adapted for television, have swelled the huge numbers of tourists in the
ancient city of Oxford, in and around which most of the
stories are set. However, those who read more than the
narrative text of a book should find in one of the Morse
novels a reason to visit a churchyard in Rugeley.

In *The Wench Is Dead* Colin Dexter describes Morse in
hospital, exercising his mind by enquiring into a historic
murder case on the local canal, and achieving a new int-
erpretation of the facts. The book is based on a real case
and a note tells careful readers that the original murder
took place in Staffordshire. In fact, its victim lies across
the road from John Parsons Cook who featured in a far
more famous Staffordshire murder. [see "What's Your
Poison"]

Christina Collins was born in Nottingham, daughter of an
inventor, and raised in comfortable circumstances. She
married a conjurer, but he died when she was in her early
thirties. Christina then married Robert Collins, an
ostler in Liverpool.

Times turned hard on Merseyside and Robert Collins went
the find work in London. He succeeded, and in June 1839
sent his wife a sovereign to pay her fare to join him.

Railway connections to London existed, though the trains
were horribly uncomfortable. Stagecoaches were frequent
but not very comfortable and quite expensive. There was,
however, another way which was relatively fast, comfortable
and not ruinously expensive - the canal boat. These carried
passengers either as fly boats travelling faster than heavy
freight boats, or as cabin boats, which were fast freights
with a passenger cabin. It was by boat that Mrs Collins
booked passage to London, paying 16 shillings (80p).

From Liverpool she took a fly boat up the Leeds & Liverpool Canal to Preston (we are told) where she transferred
to Pickford's cabin boat for the journey across the Midlands on the Trent & Mersey Canal. The crew comprised

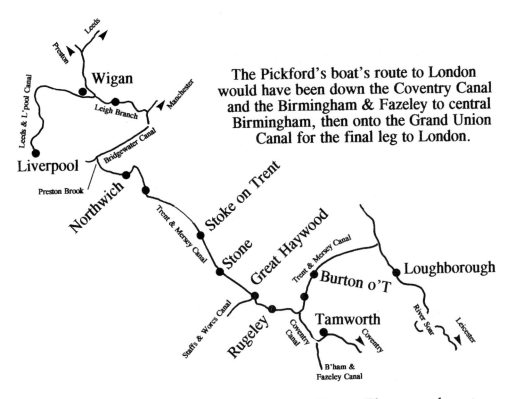

The Pickford's boat's route to London would have been down the Coventry Canal and the Birmingham & Fazeley to central Birmingham, then onto the Grand Union Canal for the final leg to London.

her captain, James Owen, two crewmen, George Thomas and William Ellis, and a 14 year old boy, William Muston.

What we are told about Christina Collins' itinery seems odd and may simply be inaccurate. To join the Trent & Mersey Canal from Liverpool the obvious route would have been along the Leeds & Liverpool to Wigan, and then the Leigh Branch and the Bridgewater Canal to the T & M at Preston Brook. The town of Preston lies far north of Wigan on the Lancaster Canal and there would have been no reason for Christina to go there. For certain, she took a fly boat to Preston Brook, which is no more than an isolated canal junction near Runcorn.

Through Harecastle Tunnel, nearly 2 miles long, the crew legged the boat, that is, they lay on planks at the boat's sides, walking along the tunnel wall to keep the boat moving. It was hard, thirsty work on a midsummer day and the crew soon began to replenish their lost fluids.

By noon the boat lay at Stoke on Trent discharging and receiving cargo. This done, the crew apart from the boy made for a tavern, where the captain alone downed three quarts of ale and a pint of porter. A gallon of ale was carried on board so that they would not run dry in the next leg of the journey, 4 miles to Barlaston and the Plume of Feathers Inn. While they stopped at Barlaston, Pickford's agent spoke to Mrs Collins in the cabin. He thought that she seemed anxious and enquired of her safety.

From Barlaston the boat moved on to Stone. By now the crew were hungry as well as thirsty and took a little food with their ale. The nervous Christina left the cabin and walked ahead along the towpath to Aston Lock, where the boat caught her up and she returned on board. The lock keeper was also concerned for her safety.

Darkness fell, but the boat slid on along the canal, coming around midnight to Hoo Mill Lock just north of Great Haywood, to the east of Stafford. The lock keeper's wife heard a woman crying and calling out on board the boat, and shouted from her bedroom window to ask what was the trouble. Captain Owen reassured her that nothing was amiss and that his lady passenger had her husband with her.

Again the boat slipped on through the summer dark, passing the steps that connected the Wolseley Road Pumping Station at Rugeley with the canal, and coming to King's Bromley. There a very drunk captain reported that a female passenger had committed suicide. She had, he said, leapt into the canal, calling out her husband's name.

Unknown to Owen, a northbound boat had already retrieved Christina's body close to the steps at Rugeley, up which she was carried ashore. The incident gave them the name "The Bloody Steps" though there was no blood. Christina had been raped and had drowned. A party of police waited for Owen's boat at Fazeley, near Tamworth and arrested its crew for rape and murder.

The trial of the captain and his crewmen took place at Stafford Assizes. William Muston turned Queen's Evidence and, though Owen vainly tried to convince the Jury of his suicide tale, all three men were convicted and sentenced to hang.

An enormous crowd gathered before dawn to witness the hanging, and were noisily disappointed when a reprieve of Ellis was announced. As his former drinking companions choked on the gallows, he was sent to begin a sentence of transportation.

Christina's body was laid to rest in Rugeley, under a memorial paid for by the townspeople. Its inscription says "In memory of this unfortunate woman who had been so barbarously treated". She and Robert Collins had no children, but both had siblings. In recent years both families have, independently, researched their history and discovered the sad story of Christina. Visiting her grave separately, they were put in touch with each other and have since visited it jointly.

The Bloody Steps have been replaced, but the new ones bear the same name, as local wags sometimes illustrate with red paint. On 17th June 1939, the centenary of the murder, a ghost was seen at the steps. It was a man in breeches and stockings with long hair tied back, walking across the water to the steps. Was it Collins, come too late to save his wife? Or Captain Owen?

Inspector Morse did not form any fresh conclusions about this particular case. Although Colin Dexter based *The Wench is Dead* upon it, he changed several of the facts, extended the life of one character and moved the action forward to 1858. All this was to create an ingenious plot revolving around a clever and ruthless fraud. There was nothing clever about the drunken, sordid murder of Christina Collins.

Major Roy Farren

We Shall Go After Him
(Codsall, Wolverhampton, Staffs 1948)

Of two unsolved murders thousands of miles apart, one may not have been a murder, the other certainly was; one led to the trial of what was possibly the wrong man, in the other there was no arrest.

The story begins in what was once called Palestine. Britain took the area from Turkey in World War I, largely through the efforts of Lawrence of Arabia who united the wandering Arab tribes against their Turkish rulers by promising independence. Unfortunately a British Prime Minister, Balfour, had promised that the Jews (yet another group of itinerant tribes from the area) should have a national home there, so the Arabs did not get their independence.

In the 1920s Palestine was made a League of Nations Mandate with Britain as the protecting power, one that by then was unloved by both Jews and Arabs. Some limited Jewish immigration was allowed but there was contant pressure to allow more, which increased following Hitler's persecution. Arabs saw the immigration as a betrayal by Britain. Inter-racial violence developed with the Jews supported by the Jewish lobby in the USA, watched by a government which was happy to see the British Empire further weakened. The Arabs raised funds from neighbouring Arab states and received advice from Nazi trainers. The Jewish groups were armed by the USA and trained by ex-British Army men.

A conference in 1946 recommended partition of Palestine into Jewish and Arab states, which infuriated Arabs and intensified the flood of Jewish immigration, much of which was illegal. The Arabs were rioting and the Jewish terrorist organisations attacked the British, with 94 dead and 53 injured in the bombing of the King David Hotel alone. On 7th August 1946 Britain announced a bar on all Jewish immigration.

In March of 1947 military law was declared in several areas. On 4th May Jewish terrorists blew open Acre Prison, releasing 251 prisoners as a reprisal for the hanging there of four members of the Stern Gang, the most violent of the Jewish groups.

Two days later on the evening of 6th May, a Jewish youth handed a felt hat in to a synagogue. He claimed that about 8.00 pm he had seen a man chase an unidentified Jewish youth and push him into a car, which sped off. He described the man as wearing tennis shoes, slacks and a military shirt, together with the hat which fell off during the incident. The sweatband was marked with partly illegible marks, appearing to be " - - F A R".

News of the alleged incident spread and another youth called at the synagogue. He was the brother of a boy called Alexander Rubowitz and believed, for what reason we do not know, that Alexander was the kidnapped boy.

The Jewish press demanded action and accused an English officer, Major Roy Farran, who commanded a group of Palestine Police. Farran and his subordinates appeared on identification parades in front of youths who said they had witnessed the incident. None were identified, but another officer was picked out.

Alexander Rubowitz's brother then tried to have Farran arrested, but the Magistrate refused. Rubowitz applied to the High Court for an order that the magistrate should justify his refusal. That, too, was refused, but the Court commented on the time taken by the military to resolve the matter.

Stung perhaps by the High Court's comments, the Army charged Farran with the boy's murder, despite the lack of a body or any evidence against him. Farran began to fear that he was being victimised and at one point removed himself to Syria. Brought back to Palestine, he was advised by his commanding officer, Colonel Labouchere, to write out a statement of his case so that he could be properly advised about his defence. He did so, still fearing a frame up since Jewish papers were saying he had been picked out on the identity parades. He escaped from his escort by leaping over the bar of the Officers' Mess and vanished.

If his second escape was remarkable, it was only a further exploit by a remarkable young man. Major Roy Alexander Farran was 26 years old in 1947 and had already collected

a Distinguished Service Order, three Military Crosses,
the French Croix de Guerre and the American Legion of
Honour. Commissioned Second Lieutenant in the Third
Carabineers in 1940, he had fought with resistance movements in Belgium, France, Germany and Burma and been
wounded four times. In May 1947 he was a Captain in the
Third King's Own Hussars attached to the first battalion
of the Irish Guards, seconded to the Palestine Police with
the acting rank of Major. Presumably his presence in Palestine was because of his practical experience of under-
ground warfare.

Ten days after his dramatic disappearance he surrendered
himself and, on 1st October 1947, appeared before a General
Court Martial charged with murdering Alexander Rubowitz
near the Jerusalem-Jericho road on the night of 6th/7th May.
The Judge Advocate was Mr Melford Stevenson KC, who
later earned a reputation as one of our most savage judges.

Opening the prosecution, Mr Maxwell Turner told how Rubowitz had been seen by his brother Jacob at their home about
6pm on 6th May. He outlined the incident between the man
and a boy that evening and stated that Alexander Rubowitz
had not been seen since. He drew attention to the grey felt
hat and the letters on the sweatband. Surprisingly, they now
appeared to read "F A R - A N", rather different from the
original " - - F A R".

Maxwell Turner went on to the morning of 7th May when
Farran had a conversation with his immediate superior, Col
Fergusson. On 3rd June the Captain (he was tried at that rank
having lost his acting rank by absence for more than twenty
one days) had told a Sergeant Faulkner that he had been
"let down". Farran had then left for Syria, but was accompanied by the Sergeant and a consrable. Farran was later
brought back by Colonel Labouchere and surrendered at
Allenby Baracks, Jerusalem on 17th June. Two days later
he compiled a notebook of press cuttings about the case
and his own comments, saying "That's that" when it was
finished. On the same night he escaped from his escort in
the Officers' Mess, but on 29th June he again gave himself
up at the camp office at Allenby Barracks.

Eighteen year old Jacob Rubowitz was called and said that on
14th May he went to a synagogue and was given the exhibited
hat. He now thought that the marking on the sweatband was
more rubbed out than when he first saw it. He confirmed his

original statement that the letters he first saw were "F A R" preceded by two illegible letters.

Jacob Jacobson, aged 13, identified Alexander Rubowitz from a photograph as the boy he had seen chased and put in a car on 6th May. He described the incident and the clothing of the pursuing man and told how he had taken the dropped hat to a synagogue. He admitted attending three identity parades without seeing anyone involved in the incident.

Moshe Keshin, a boy who had been with Jacobson, testified that he had seen the incident and that the boy had been put into a car with the registration M993. Five minutes later he saw the car again. The boy was still in it, but its registration was now M662.

Colonel Bernard Fergusson, assistant Inspector General of Palestine Police in charge of training, was called but refused to give evidence of his conversation with Farran on the morning after the incident, claiming that he might incriminate himself. Judge Advocate Melford Stevenson explained that English law protected a witness from the danger of self incrimination and Colonel Fergusson was permitted to leave, having successfully cast a deep shadow over Captain Farran.

Sergeant Faulkner confirmed the "let down" remark and explained that he had felt obliged to accompany Farran to Syria as escort and had taken a constable with them. After six days he had returned, leaving Captain Farran behind. Mr Fearnley Whittingstall, defending Counsel, asked him:

> "Did you know that the wildest rumours were being circulated about Captain Farran, and that, so far as gossip was concerned, he was not being given a chance?

> Sergeant Faulkner -- Yes, sir.

The officer in charge of the identity parades testified that Captain Farran and all his men had appeared in line and no witness had identified any of them. Press stories that Farran had been picked out were untrue. Another officer said that Jacob Rubowitz had given him the hat on 13th May. The marking on the sweatband then was "F A R - A N" but the area was now smeared and he did not know how this had happened.

There was evidence of an unsuccessful search for a body near the Jericho road and then the prosecution sought to introduce the notebook compiled by the defendant. The defence objected, on the basis that it was confidential, having been compiled with a view to instructing the Captain's legal advisors. The Court adjourned.

Next morning an "inner trial" took place to consider the admissibility of the notebook. Colonel P H Labouchere, Commanding Officer of the Third King's Own Hussars, Farran's regiment, told how he had gone to Syria and brought the Captain back to Allenby Barracks where, in the presence of a police officer, he had told Farran to regard him as his legal adviser and to write down a statement of his case. The Commanding Officer of a regiment, he said, was always a legal adviser to his officers and men, and stood in a father to son relationship with them. He had expected to receive Captain Farran's notes, but had not.

Even in the face of this evidence, the prosecution invited the Court to admit the document on the basis that it was not covered by legal privilege, having been written "to unburden his mind". That silly argument rightly failed and the notes were ruled inadmissible.

There was no further prosecution evidence and the defence offered none. Mr Fearnley Whittingstall submitted that there was no case against Farran. He and his squad had stood on identity parades in a proportion of ten of them with two strangers and not been selected. No one had sought to connect Farran with the dropped hat and, finally, no one had been convicted of murder in a British court for generations without a body or evidence of death.

The prosecutor admitted that without the notebook, there was no case against Captain Farran, and the Judge Advocate summed up, saying that no direct or circumstantial evidence showed that Rubowitz was dead and there were discrepancies around the letters on the hat. The law was clear, without evidence of killing there could be no conviction and, even if there were a confession, it could not be acted upon in the circumstances.

After fifteen minutes deliberation, the President of the Court announced a verdict of not guilty to applause from police and army personnel. The reporter for *The Times* seemed to be as suspicious of the curious part played by Colonel B Fergusson as I am, for he noted that the Colonel was to leave Palestine within days and revert to the Army, having resigned from the Palestine Police in June.

Captain Farran came home and left the Army. He set about writing a book, *The Winged Dagger,* about his wartime experiences. In Palestine the Stern Gang posted leaflets on walls, "Captain Farran's time will come. We shall go after him to the ends of the world".

In the October following his acquittal, Roy Farran was given the American Legion of Merit award. At that ceremony he revealed that he had received threatening letters at his home. Posted in the East End of London, they contained papers with "Revenge" written in Hebrew. In the same month the Rubowitz family applied for a warrant for Farran's arrest for kidnapping under the Fugitive Offenders Act. The boy witnesses who had failed to identify Farran now said that they had done so and the warrant was issued. However, the Attorney General examined the boys' evidence at the Court Martial and stayed the warrant.

Captain Farran's presence in England may have been public - ised by a Sunday newspaper article about him, in the wake of which he brought proceedings against the newspaper.

Roy Farran's home was at The Myron, Histons Hill, Codsall, Wolverhampton, where he lived with his parents and brothers. On the morning of 3rd May 1948 he was expecting his book to be published, so nobody was surprised when Postwoman Eileen Hayes delivered a parcel. Captain Farran's younger brother, 26 year old Rex, received the package and opened it, apparently thinking it was an advance copy of the book. A fierce blast shook the house and blew out windows. Rex Farran suffered terrible injuries to his lower body and thighs from which he later died.

The bomb was a fragmentation device hidden in a book of Shakespeare's works which was powered by a battery and triggered by unwrapping. The book was a widely available edition sold all over Britain and the place of purchase was never discovered. Surviving fragments of the package rev- ealed that it had been handed in at an London East End Post Office during the previous weekend. A mark on the wrapper could have been made in any of three hundred post offices.

Checks were made on aliens who might be connected with the Stern Gang, and a British news agency in Paris received a statement by telephone from a caller claiming that the Stern Gang was responsible. In a dictated statement he said that the bomb was a punishment of Captain Farran for the murder of a Jewish youth and a protest against British reinforcements sent to Palestine, though the British were to leave Palestine within days.

The bitter, bloody, tripartite war in Palestine had continued to escalate until Britain informed the United Nations that it was not prepared to impose a solution by force; if the UN or the USA would not take responsibility, Britain would surrender its mandate. For once, both Jews and Arabs welcomed the move.

British withdrawal began and was scheduled to finish by midnight 14th May 1948. Unbridled fighting between Jews and Arabs broke out. The UN had voted to partition Palestine into a Jewish state and an Arab state with a separate administration of Jerusalem. Four hours before the deadline, the Jews declared Palestine to be the Jewish state of Israel.

While the world expected the UN (or the USA on its behalf) to step in and enforce the partition decision, President Truman recognised the state of Israel. The surrounding Arab territories declared war.

In Britain the hunt for the murderers of Rex Farran reached a dead end. Roy Farran emigrated to Canada and became a successful newspaper proprietor in the Calgary area.

Two unsolved murders, or was young Rubowitz murdered? No evidence of his death was ever found. The trial of Roy Farran was a complex farrago of lies and doctored evidence behind which lay no evidence except his own statement, yet a heroic young officer was placed in deadly jeopardy. What was in the statement? Colonel Fergusson implied that Farran had admitted something illegal. The Court's officers read the notebook before declaring it inadmissible and the Judge Advocate later warned them that they must not convict where there was no proof, even if there was a confession. Was a confession in the notebook? Fifty years on, like the politics of the Middle East, the case remains unsolved and very likely insoluble.

Brief Life

(Little Stretton, Leicestershire 1919)

Murder, like other forms of death, may come at any time or
place. It does not confine itself to the country houses of one
school of fiction or the grimy cities favoured by another.

July 5th 1919 was a warm day and the lanes and hedges
of rural Leicestershire were ripe with summer and rich
with the wild flowers, that had not then been wiped out
by petrol fumes and weedkillers. Bella Wright, 21 years
old and an employee of Bates Rubber Mill, left her home
at Evington to post a letter, riding on her beloved bicycle.
After this errand she set out to visit her uncle at Gaulby.
She was young, single and pretty, nine days away from her
22nd birthday and in love with a sailor aboard HMS Diadem.
Nothing in Bella's world can have seemed wrong until she
noticed that her rear wheel was loose.

At the junction of Stoughton Lane and Gaulby Lane she dis-
mounted and tried to adjust the wheel. As she did, another
cyclist, a young man on a green bicycle, came up and offered help. She asked him for a spanner, which he had not
got, but he made what attempts he could to tighten the
wheel. When she told him that she was bound for Gaulby
he courteously offered to escort her.

They reached the home of her uncle, Mr Measures, and
Bella told her escort that she would only be ten minutes,
which he construed as an invitation to wait for her. His wait
was prolonged because Mr Measures' daughter and son in law
were visiting. They enquired about her escort and suggested
that the man on the green bicycle was too old for Bella, so
she waited for him to leave.

Eventually the stranger rode away, but at Gaulby Church he
had a puncture. By the time he had repaired it Bella had not
passed him, so he rode back to her uncle's cottage, arriving
just as Bella left. She again accepted his escort and they
cycled together through Little Stretton to the junction of
the Burton Overy road before Great Stretton.

There she told him that she must turn left, through Great Stretton, while his route lay to the right.

At about 9.20 pm a farmer, Mr Cowell, came along the Gartree Road from Great Stretton and found Bella Wright. The girl and her bicycle were lying in the lane to Little Stretton, near a field gate by the junction. He examined her and found that she was dead, so he went to his farm at Little Stretton, harnessed his trap and made for Great Glen to report to Constable Hall and Doctor Williams.

Darkness had fallen by the time the doctor arrived at the scene, and he had Bella's body taken to an empty house nearby. It was assumed that she had died in a cycling accident.

In the daylight of the next morning, Sunday, PC Hall returned to the scene and searched it carefully. In the lane he found the corpse of a blood smeared carrion crow, whose bloody footprints were also in evidence. He assumed that the creature had seized the opportunity of feasting on Bella's body and had gorged itself to death. He was rather more surprised to find a .455 revolver bullet in the road.

Hall went to the empty house, where he washed the blood from Bella's face to reveal that she had been shot dead by a bullet passing right through the head. A full post mortem by Doctor Williams and another doctor confirmed this finding, and the case became a murder enquiry.

The story of the man with the green bicycle soon emerged, but not his identity. On 7th July the Police issued a handbill carrying a description of the man as 35-40 years old 5'7" to 5'9" tall, clean shaven, broad faced and broad built with a squeaky voice. His bicycle was described as a green framed gents' BSA with upturned handle bars and an unusual back pedalling brake.

Despite the descriptions, the man was not found. On the 11th July Bella was buried at Stoughton Church to the hymns *Brief Life is Here Our Portion, Peace, Perfect Peace* and *Rest in the Lord*.

The hunt for the wanted cyclist continued without success until 23rd February 1920, when a bargee on the canal near Leicester gasworks found his tow rope snagged on something

LEICESTERSHIRE CONSTABULARY.

£5 REWARD.

At 9-20 p.m., 5th instant, the body of a woman, since identified as that of ANNIE BELLA WRIGHT, was found lying on the Burton Overy Road, Stretton Parva, with a bullet wound through the head, and her bicycle lying close by.

Shortly before the finding of the body the deceased left an adjacent village in company of a man of the following description :—

Age 35 to 40 years, height 5 ft. 7 in. to 5 ft. 9 in.; apparently usually clean shaven, but had not shaved for a few days, hair turning grey, broad full face, broad build, said to have squeaking voice and to speak in a low tone.

Dressed in light Rainproof Coat with green plaid lining, grey mixture jacket suit, grey cap, collar and tie, black boots, and wearing cycle clips.

Had bicycle of following description, *viz.*:—Gent's B.S.A., green enamelled frame, black mudguards, usual plated parts, up-turned handle bar, 3-speed gear, control lever on right of handle bar, lever front brake, back-pedalling brake worked from crank and of unusual pattern, open centre gear case, *Brooke's* saddle with spiral springs of wire cable. The 3-speed control had recently been repaired with length of new cable.

Thorough enquiries are earnestly requested at all places where bicycles are repaired.

If met with the man should be detained, and any information either of the man or the bicycle wired or telephoned to E. HOLMES, ESQ., CHIEF CONSTABLE OF COUNTY, LEICESTER, or to SUPT L BOWLEY, COUNTY POLICE STATION, LEICESTER.

County Constabulary Office,
Leicester, 7th July, 1919.

T H JEAYS & SONS. PRINTERS 7 ST. MARTINS. LEICESTER.

under the water. A few tugs revealed a gent's BSA bicycle with a green enamelled frame and its rear wheel missing. Dragging the canal produced from the same area a revolver holster containing .455 cartridges. The serial number of the cycle frame soon led the police to a man named Ronald Vivian Light.

Light was then a 35 year old teacher in Cheltenham. Born in Leicester, he had graduated as a civil engineer at Birmingham University before working for the Midland Railway at Derby and for a firm in Buxton. He had bought the green bike in the summer of 1910. In the Great War Light had been commissioned second lieutenant in the Royal Engineers and served overseas. However, in August 1916 he had left them to join the Honourable Artillery Company as a private, and in September was sent abroad once more. Light returned from the War seriously shell shocked and had spent time in several hospitals in Britain refore being discharged in January 1919. At the time of Bella's death he had been living with his mother in Leicester.

Light was questioned and at first denied any knowledge of the matter. He said that he had not owned the bicycle or a revolver, that the holster was not his and that he had not been cycling near Gaulby on 5th July. However, the bike was traceable to him and it was established that like thousands of soldiers, he had brought a .455 revolver back from the War. Light changed his mind and admitted that he had owned the bicycle but had sold it - to a "man in a pub". He changed his mind again and remembered that he had owned a revolver, but that had gone the same way as the cycle. He was charged with the murder of Bella Wright and committed for trial.

His trial began at Leicester Castle on 20th June 1920 when he was defended by Sir Edward Marshall Hall, KC. The prosecution mounted an impressive panoply of circumstantial evidence - the bicycle, the holster, the cartridges and, most of all, Ronald Light's lies and evasions. The handbill issued two days after Bella's death had convinced the public that the man on the green bicycle was Bella Wright's killer and Light's chances of acquital looked small.

Nevertheless, the Crown over reached itself in suggesting that the motive was lust. If so, why had not Light bent the girl to his purposes by threatening her with the pistol and then shot her afterwards? In addition, the prosecution argued that Bella had been shot at close range.

Marshall Hall, a superstar among defending advocates, called Light and, on oath he admitted his lies. He told how he had left home for a cycle ride on 5th July and of meeting the girl, how they met again and separated in the Burton Overy road. He knew nothing about her death until the following Tuesday, by which time the highly prejudicial handbill was circulating. There had been no witness to his parting with Bella and he owned a .455 revolver. Seized by panic he had first hidden the bicycle then, in October, had removed the rear wheel with its distinctive brake and thrown the gun, holster, cartridges and bicycle into the canal. Inability to est-ablish his innocence had led him to lie to the police.

Light's apparent frankness made a good impression on the jury, but Marshall Hall had an ace up his sleeve. His speciality was firearms and he understood, as the prosecution apparently did not, the nature of a .455 bullet. He carried out experiments and called Robert Churchill, the eminent gunsmith, to support his case. Churchill explained that a .455 bullet is a very large missile (far bigger, for example, than the American 357 Magnum beloved of Dirty Harry) Fired at close range it would not have passed neatly through Bella's head to land 5 yards away, but would have blown half her head away on exit and continued for some distance.

Ronald Vivian Light was acquitted. He removed to Kent and died there, aged almost 90, in 1975. The famous bi-cycle was tracked down by a modern researcher to the wall of a cycle shop in Leicestershire where, so far as I know, it still hangs.

You may, if you ignore the absence of motive and the ballistic evidence, believe that Ronald Light was lucky and got away with it through the skills of a great advocate. Or you may wonder how Bella Wright came to die.

Cast your mind back to the scene that PC Hall found on that summer Sunday morning; the dead girl's blood on the road, a spent bullet, bloody claw marks and the corpse of a blood boltered crow. In the wake of the Great War .455 pistols and the ammunition for them were commonplace. Had someone set out on that bright summer evening of July 5th to shoot crows, with a shotgun loaded with .455 ammunition, as can be done? Did he aim at a crow perched on a gate and shoot just as a luckless girl rode into the line of fire? The ammunition does not fit tightly into a shotgun barrel and would have lost much of its normal velocity.

Accidental death, like murder, comes at any time or place. Did somebody go to his grave knowing that he shot Bella Wright by accident, or is there an old man somewhere who still carries that burden?

While There's A Country Lane
(Rushall, Walsall, Staffs 1941)

In September 1941, two years into World War Two, Britain is still alone in her struggle with Hitler's Germany. All of Western Europe opposite our coast is under Nazi domination and America is still not involved in the armed conflict. In the Midlands the factories are working as never before to strengthen the sinews of war. Weapons, equipment, machinery, aircraft, vehicles, and components for all of them are pouring out of Midland plants.

In the great urban sprawl that houses the factories and their workers at the heart of the region, the men and women who are working night and day listen to radio music as they toil:

>"There'll always be an England,
> while there's a country lane,
> wherever there's a cottage small
> beside a field of grain."

The saving grace of Britain's industrial towns has always been the fact that somewhere, not so very far from lowering factories and grey terraced streets there really are country walks among meadows and pools. One of them is still there, almost exactly as it was more than half a century ago.

Leave Walsall by the Lichfield road and turn off at Rushall into the lane that leads to Saint Michael's Church. Just past the church the lane ends at a gate. To the right behind the church lies Rushall Manor, besieged in the Civil War, and beyond it are flooded limepits now popular with anglers. Left from the gate a track strikes across the meadow to disappear under a railway bridge, known as the "Cattle Bridge".

It was noon on Sunday, 21st September 1941, and two young women were strolling on that track to the Cattle Bridge. They were 24 year old Violet Richards and 18 year old Kitty Lyon, both from Paddock in South Walsall.

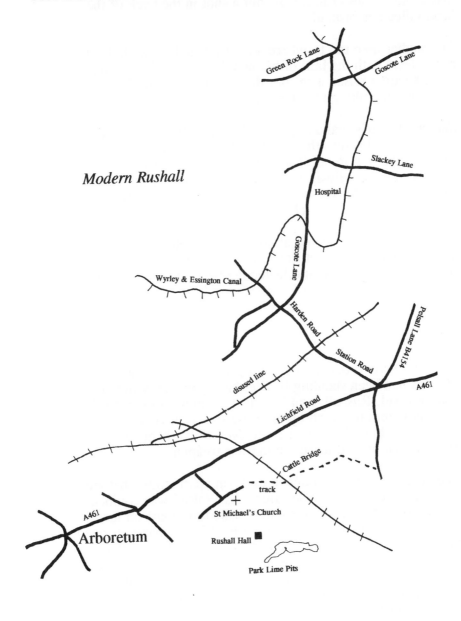

As they walked under the bridge they passed a lone soldier standing in the arch. Soldiers were a commonplace so they took little notice, except to see that though in uniform, he wore no cap.

They had walked on a few yards when a shot rang out and Violet fell, struck in the back by a bullet that passed right through her. Young Kitty saw the soldier was holding a pistol and ran away in terror, but a shot in the back of the head killed her instantly.

The soldier then ran to where Violet lay and began to beat at her head with the butt of his pistol. She tried to protect herself with a raised arm, but the savage blows broke it. He went on striking at her head until she lay still.

Seizing the girls' handbags the killer ran off. From Cattle Bridge he fled across the fields to the Lichfield Road and made for Station Road. There he climbed the fence and went beside the railway track, pausing only to drop something. Heading for Goscote he passed the Isolation Hospital and arrived at Green Rock Lane.

The girls were discovered about one hour later. From Walsall's Goodall Street Police Station came Detective Inspector Greenhough and Detective Sergeant Sam Dallow. When they arrived at the Cattle Bridge Violet Richards was semi conscious, despite the bullet and the beating. She was able to tell them, "It was a soldier", before being rushed to Walsall's Sister Dora Hospital.

Enquiries soon produced two valuable clues. Mr Thomas Thomas had been standing beside the railway crossing at Station Road, Rushall, and had seen a hatless soldier drop something into the ditch by the railway fence. A search revealed a .45 calibre service revolver with a bent trigger guard which proved to be the murder weapon.

The description of a soldier in uniform apart from a hat led to a search for an Army deserter. As Walsall was combed for deserters and Army units were asked to report on men from the town who were absent without leave, panic gripped those deserters who were in the area. Retired police officers still tell how a queue stretched from Goodall Street Police Station down the Market Place as men surrendered themselves to be shipped back to their units, rather than risk suspicion of murder.

Violet Richards could not give a more detailed description of the man who had attacked her and murdered her friend, and no individual suspect came to light. After a few days the Chief Constable of Walsall Borough Police called in Scotland Yard, and Detective Superintendent Arthur Davies and Detective Sergeant Sidney Powell arrived.

Routine enquiries by the Army showed that a Walsall man, Private Douglas Peach, had been AWOL but had returned to his unit and was in military custody. He was brought to Walsall and questioned, but denied all knowledge of the incident.

However, it was soon discovered that a .45 revolver was missed from Peach's unit at a time when he was in custody, and he might well have been able to steal it from the guard room. A witness remembered that Peach had showed him a revolver and bragged that he carried it because he was a member of the "Secret Police", pointing to an "SP" badge on his left arm. The letters just meant "Special Proficiency" in shooting. Taken all together, the police believed that Peach was their man. He was brought back to Walsall and charged with the murder of Kitty Lyon and the attempted murder of Violet Richards.

At the committal proceedings in Walsall's Guildhall, Violet Richards gave her evidence from a stretcher. Beaten with the pistol until its trigger guard bent, suffering a broken skull, she nevertheless remembered the assault and clearly identified Douglas Peach as the attacker. Peach was committed for trial at Stafford and appeared before the Assizes on 26th November 1941. Found guilty, he was executed at Winson Green, the last Walsall man to suffer that fate.

The Sister Dora Hospital is gone, replaced by a block of flats on a corner of Wednesbury Road. The old Guildhall and the Goodall Street Police Station stand unused, but the Cattle Bridge and the track leading to it are still there, exactly as they were on that Sunday when Douglas Peach killed one girl and beat another for the few shillings in their handbags.

A Man That Is A Wizard
(Lower Quinton, Warks 1945)

Travel down the A34 from Birmingham towards Oxford and, just before you reach the border between Warwickshire and Oxfordshire, you will come to Long Compton. Nothing could be more English than the little villages of that area, and Long Compton is no exception. You half expect to see Miss Marple walking along the main street, or the Famous Five setting out for a holiday picnic.

However, Long Compton has a darker side. On New Year's Day in 1876 the *Illustrated Police News* reported what it called a "singular case of murder" from the village. James Haywood, a 40 year old farm hand had appeared at Warwick Assizes charged with the murder of 80 year old Anne Tennant at Long Compton where, said that high minded newspaper,"it was proved in evidence that fully one third of the villagers believed in witchcraft".

The report went on:

> " The prisoner, believing in the common superstition, stabbed the deceased, who was eighty years of age, with a pitchfork, under the impression that she was one of the fifteen witches he ought to kill. It was admitted that on all other subjects he was sane. He justified his conduct by referring to verses from Leviticus: - 'A man also or woman that hath a familiar spirit, or that is a wizard, should be put to death'......The judge said that such a prevalence of this superstition would be disgraceful to savages."

Haywood was found insane and confined during Her Majesty's pleasure, but it would take more than a Judge's scorn to wipe out the belief in witchcraft from that area.

Carry on down the A34 and you will soon climb the hill on top of which the Rollright Stones stand. This four thousand year old megalithic circle is flanked by an outlier, the King's Stone, and the remains of a chambered tomb, the Whispering Knights. Whatever rites were practised by the builders of the Rollrights, as recently as 1995 a young woman was telling the national press that, in the 1970s, she was forced to take part in sex and magic rituals at the Stones, in which tramps and child runaways were sacrificed. Her story may well not be true but, as in Haywood's case, it may be that what matters is what you believe.

A few miles north-west of the Rollrights lies Lower Quinton, in Warwickshire, another quintessentially English village. In its churchyard lies Charles Walton who lived in a nearby cottage. At 74 years of age he suffered from rheumatism but continued working as a labourer.

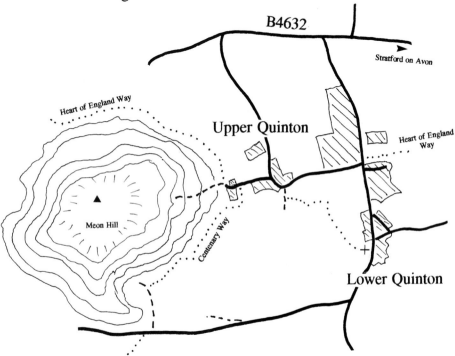

On 14th February 1945 the old man set out with hayfork and trouncing hook to do some hedging for Farmer Potter in a field on the flank of Meon Hill. This distinctively sculpted northern outlier of the Cotswolds is only 215 feet high, but its crest was an Iron Age fort and it looms over the village and the level Avon plain.

Charles Walton's niece, who looked after him, gave him a piece of fruitcake for his lunch and then set off for her own work. She knew that when the short day grew dark, her uncle would come home and eat the meal she had left for him before she returned about 6 o'clock.

When the niece returned home she found the food uneaten and Walton was nowhere to be seen. Afraid that her uncle might have fallen and been unable to rise, she went to her neighbour, Harry Beasley, and together they set out to see Walton's employer, Alfred Potter at Firs Farm. He told them he believed he had seen Charles Walton working up on Meon Hill at about lunchtime,

Taking a torch, the three went up to the field, calling out for the old man as they went. There was no response and eventually the torch revealed why not. Charles Walton lay on his back near the hedge that he had been trimming. He had not fallen from his rheumatics, but been cut down and beaten.

Despite his age and infirmity, the old labourer had fought for his life. His arms were slashed where he had defended himself, his head was battered and his own trouncing hook was still embedded in his throat. His body was pinned to the ground by a hayfork, driven with such force that its two prongs had passed through Walton's face and neck and 6 inches into the ground. Its handle was firmly wedged into the hedge. Walton's clothing was disarranged, his braces broken, his buttons undone and his cheap old watch had been snatched from its chain in his waistcoat pocket. Close to him lay his walking stick, matted with blood and hair, evidently one of the weapons of attack.

His throat and chest had been slashed with cuts in the form of a cross.

Police soon arrived, and it took two officers to pull out the pitchfork so that the body could be removed. Warwickshire's Detective Superintendent Alec Spooner was put in charge of the case, but Scotland Yard was soon asked for assistance. Detective Superintendent Robert Fabian and Sergeant Albert Webb arrived in the Midlands and Superintendent Spooner soon showed them a book, *Folklore, Old Customs and Superstitions in Shakespeareland*, written in 1929 by the erstwhile vicar of nearby Whitchurch. It contained an account of the murder of Anne Tennant at Long Compton in 1875 with a reference to a ploughboy who in 1885 met a black dog on his way home from work. Nine times he met the strange dog, a creature which represents evil in Warwickshire folklore. On the ninth day it turned into a headless woman, and the next day he was told of the death of his sister. The lad's name was Charles Walton.

KILLING A SUPPOSED WITCH

Spooner was not done. Another book, *Warwickshire* by Clive Holland, published in 1906, had a further description of the murder of Anne Tennant, where it was explained that the use of a pitchfork in killing a witch was a relic of the old Anglo-Saxon "Stacung" or "sticking". It was believed to be the only effective way to kill a witch and neutralise any current spells. John Hayward's explanation was quoted;

> "I pinned her to the ground with a hayfork before slashing her throat with a bill hook in the form of a cross."

Fabian was sceptical. In his long and successful career in London he had little or nothing to do with witchcraft. He later described himself as bringing the 20th century to Lower Quinton "like a cold shower bath". Bob Fabian believed in simpler motives for murder and set out to find one.

As a matter of routine the detectives examined the old man's life. Charles Walton was born in Lower Quinton in 1870, fourth of a family of six. In his thirties he lodged with the family of a farm bailiff in Upper Quinton and courted their daughter, Lucy Hughes. In 1912 Walton's mother died, and in the following year he suddenly abandoned Lucy and went to Stratford upon Avon to marry his 31 year old cousin.

local opinion was that he had behaved badly by Lucy because his cousin had inherited a few hundreds of pounds
from her own mother.

Walton returned to Lower Quinton with his wife, bringing
with them her niece, 3 year old Edith. Her mother had also
died recently and the Waltons were to care for her. Mrs
Walton was not a hearty woman and died in 1927, leaving
Charles £297, a small fortune to a farm labourer.

The question of money soon began to suggest a motive for
the murder of Charles Walton. He had been a careful man
who lived frugally. His inheritance from his wife had gone
into a building society and he must have added to it, for he
had always worked and was still doing so in his 70s. The
rent of his cottage was only 3 shillings (15p) weekly and his
niece supported herself. Nevertheless, at his death he had
only £2/11/9d (£2.60p) in the bank, £1/10s (£1.50p) at
home and the same sum in an old purse.

Some people recalled him wearing a money belt, described as stuffed with paper money. Others said that he didn't
carry much money. Someone remembered him saying that
he was "worth a few hundreds" just before his death. He
certainly should have been. Where was it?

The police checked on the old man's movements on his last
day, such as they were. Farmer Potter seemed to be the only
source of information. He said that he had been in a village
pub that morning with another farmer. They had arrived
about 11.45 am, had a quick drink and left about noon,
standing in the street to talk for about ten minutes before
separating. Potter had returned to Firs Farm and carried
out various jobs, including giving hay to his cattle. While
walking in his fields he had seen what he thought was Walton
at work in the distance. He thought it was Walton, as no one
else was likely to have been cutting hedges on Potter's land
in his shirt sleeves. Oddly, Charles Walton had no shirt
sleeves on the day he died, he was working in a shirt with
the sleeves completely cut off.

The murder scene provided no clues. It had been well tramp-
led in the dark when Edith, Harry Beasley and Potter found
the body, and Potter had even seized the pitch fork with the
intention of pulling it free.

The villagers were close mouthed and told the London detectives little, but a picture began to emerge of a man who was not an average labourer. Charles Walton was the ploughboy who had seen the black dog in 1885, and his psychic career had not ended there.

The missing watch was a cheap one in a tin case, but had contained a disc of black glass. According to some, Walton used it as a "scrying glass", an aid to concentration like a crystal ball when trying to see the future. Other villagers feared that Walton had used his powers against people, perhaps for money.

The old man had been thought odd by his neighbours, rarely drinking in the village pub and preferring to buy cider, sometimes as much as 12 gallons at a time, and taking it home by wheelbarrow to drink in solitude.

The date of his death contributed to the idea that it was connected with witchcraft. It occurred on 14th February, which to most Britons is just St Valentine's Day, but is said to be much more significant to practitioners of the "old religion".

When our calendar was regulated in the 18th century eleven days needed to be removed to eliminate accumulated errors. Traditionalists clung to the "Old Style", continuing their celebrations on the equivalent date to the original festival. So for example, there is a part of Scotland where Christmas is still celebrated on 6th January, eleven days away from 25th December.

St Valentine's Day falls, according to some, eleven days after Imbolc, the old Celtic pagan festival of returning light which was (is?) celebrated by some witch covens as a "Witches Sabbat". There is a difficulty here for the real difference between Imbolc and St Valentine's Day is twelve days, not eleven. Nevertheless, a Birmingham woman later claimed she knew Walton had been sacrificed by a coven, his killer being brought to the area by car. The celebrated Egyptologist Dr Margaret Murray examined the ritual poss- ibilities of the case, and the American Dr Margaret Mead, whose studies were mainly of primitive societies in remote places, visited Lower Quinton.

Fabian must have resisted all this ancient, rural, folklore with every rational fibre of a Metropolitan detective's being. He had every villager questioned, then extended the questioning to visitors, tinkers, even a tramp in the West of England. Samples of hair, blood and soil were sent for analysis. The Royal Air Force at Leamington carried out a photographic flight over Lower Quinton. Special Branch interpreters were brought in to question hundreds of prisoners of war in a nearby camp.

A breakthrough seemed possible when a witness reported seeing a bloodstained man huddled in a ditch on 14th February and an Italian prisoner of war informed on a fellow prisoner who had been seen urgently removing blood from his clothing. It transpired that the bloodstained Italian had been supplementing the camp diet by poaching and the blood came from a rabbit.

Despite Fabian's efforts at rational detection, the suggestion of witchcraft kept reasserting itself. One day as he walked in the village, he was passed by a large black dog. Shortly afterwards he saw a young boy and asked him if he was looking for the dog. The boy told him he hadn't seen any dog and ran away. On another occasion the corpse of a black dog was found hanging from the willow tree where Charles Walton had died.

Still the people of Lower Quinton would not talk and, in the end their silence defeated the brilliant "Fabian of the Yard". Other cases called him, and he and Sergeant Webb left for London. The investigation wound down and the file was not closed, but put away. Superintendent Spooner felt keenly the failure to solve a murder on his patch. For nineteen years afterwards he would return to Lower Quinton on St Valentine's Day, take a drink in the village pub and climb Meon Hill to stand by the willow tree and gaze over the village, letting the locals know that he had not forgotten and that he was still waiting for someone to talk. The villagers responded by naming the tree "Spooner's Willow", but they did not talk. Spooner gave up his annual vigil and retired.

It has been said that the concluding paragraph of the Lower Quinton story will never be written, but that is not necessarily true. As Superintendent Spooner knew, time passes and secrets leak out. More than fifty years has passed and it is possible to review the whole case and consider the possibility that the police were misled by the folkloric aspects of the case. Lower Quinton (and, apparently Walton himself) believed Walton to be psychic and maybe maliciously so, a witch or wizard in country terms. Clive Holland's comments on the 1875 case showed that the effective neutralisation of a witch's powers involved killing in the prescribed way, and that was how Charles Walton was killed.

However, that does not mean that Walton was killed because he was a witch. It may mean only that the killer knew or believed that the old man had paranormal powers and in killing him, feared those powers.

The silence of the villagers after the death of a man that some of them feared was unusual. Normally that is the point at which tongues begin to wag, unless there is someone else that they fear more, someone who has killed brutally once and might do so again. Common sense says that the killer was a local man, a man because of the strength necessary to drive that pitchfork into the ground, and local because Walton had not left the area in years. Whatever the cause of his death it arose in Lower Quinton and no one imported a hitman or woman.

There was quite a large sum of money missing and Charles Walton's watch was taken, but it was not snatched from its chain because he kept his scrying glass in it. Indeed, one account of the case says that the glass was left at home. The watch case was a useful place to keep something important, like the scrying glass. If it was left at home it would be because it had been replaced by something equally or more important. If it was not left at home, perhaps it shared the case with something else, something very thin. A piece of paper? An IOU for money borrowed?

The village knew that Walton had money but he did not seem to have friends. To whom would he have lent a large sum? Surely only someone with whom he had some kind of relationship and definitely someone he thought could pay him back. What would he have done if they didn't pay? Might he have threatened them with his alleged powers, provoking both the deadly attack and the precautions against spells? When the deed was done, wouldn't the murdering debtor tear away the watchcase so as to remove the IOU?

Who had a relationship with Charles Walton of any length? Who might he have thought could repay him? Who knew where he was on 14th February 1945? Who had a perfect excuse for being in the same place as Walton? Who laid hold of the pitchfork so that there was an explanation if any fingerprint was found on it? Who knew how to prevent a dead witch harming him? Who might hang a dog on a tree to mislead the police?

Finish your journey to rural Warwickshire by looking at the handsome house that stands opposite Lower Quinton church. It was once three miserable cottages and Charles Walton paid his 3 shillings for the one on the right. Look over the churchyard where the old man lies, accompanied now by his employer, Farmer Potter. Then have a drink in the Gay Dog pub and ask the locals if they think Farmer Potter killed Charles Walton. Don't be surprised if they won't talk to you any more than they talked to Spooner or Fabian.

The present state of the cottages where Charles Walton lived for 15p a week half a century ago.

I Didn't Want To Upset Anybody
(Edgbaston, Birmingham 1959)

"Have you noticed", they always ask in the pub, the shop
or at work, "how these things always happen close to Christmas?", and they continue discussing the latest train crash,
plane wreck or murder. Sometimes one has to wonder if
it is a law of nature that TV and the tabloids should have
tragedy headlines at Christmas. There are more accidents,
more marital breakdowns, more suicides and more murders
around that time than any other.

More people travel at Christmas, so there are extra trains
and planes. More people drink more at Christmas, so there
is more drunkenness. More people feel the sting of want or
family breakdown at Christmas, so there is more raw emotion,
and as whole, secure families gather for the festival, more
outsiders feel increased loneliness. Sometimes they stop even
trying to keep a foothold in society and take their own lives.
Sometimes, as at Christmas 1959, the darkness within them
explodes outwards, bringing tragedy to themselves and others.

Birmingham's Christmas horror began as far back as March
1959. At 11.15 pm one night the porter had just finished his
rounds at the YWCA Hostel in Wheeley's Road, Edgbaston.
"Edencroft", the hostel occupied one of the large houses that
the manufacturers and professional men of Birmingham once
built in this spacious, wealthy suburb. Apart from the big
house itself, a single storey annexe housed further rooms
and a laundry. In one of the annexe bedrooms a young
teacher was about to doze off.

Suddenly the light went on and a dark figure entered the
room. "Hello", it said, "I'm looking for Kathleen Ryan".
Trying desperately to keep calm, the frightened girl asked
the man how he got in. Through the window, he told her,
and moved towards the bed. "Please", she said, "I'm engaged to be married. Perhaps you'd better be going".

Miraculously, it worked. The intruder turned to the door
and the courageous girl jumped out of bed, led the man
to the front door and let him out. Moments later she
phoned the police, but they could find no sign of him.

Nine months later on the evening of 23rd December 1959, 21 year old Margaret Brown was using the hostel laundry. Most of the girls had already left Edencroft to spend Christmas at home, and Margaret was preparing to travel.

It was a damp, cold night and as she ironed her clothes Margaret felt a draught. She closed a door to the adjacent washroom, but as she returned to her ironing, it clicked open again. Once more she closed it but the same thing happened.

Margaret had returned to the washroom to close the door yet again, when the lights went out. She had only a glimpse of a figure before she was struck on the head. Luckily she remained conscious and screamed again and again, and the intruder fled.

As in March the police were called, but this time gained a description of the attacker. Margaret said he was about 28 years old, 5'8" tall with a ruddy complexion and well defined chin. Casts were taken from footprints found outside the window and a full check made of the hostel buildings.

The room next to the scene of the March incident was locked, but looking through a chink in the curtains, an officer saw a pair of naked, motionless legs on the floor. The door of the room was smashed open and one officer vomited when he saw what lay inside. It was the headless body of 29 year old Sidney Stephanie Baird.

Detective Chief Superintendent Haughton of Birmingham CID took charge of the case. He closed the perimeter of the City with roadblocks, flashed details to every police force in Britain and to Interpol, and issued statements to press, radio and television news. A police dog was brought to the hostel and began to follow the killer's trail, but a road accident flung the contents of a truck across a road and wiped out the scent.

The decapitation of Stephanie and the hideous mutilations done to her suggested that her murderer have been widely bloodstained, and Haughton appealed for sightings of a bloodstained man. In the meantime he kept from the media the finding on Stephanie's dressing table of a scribbled note which read:

" This is the thing I Tought (sic) would never come."

Bus conductor William Humphries told the Police that his bus had been boarded near the YWCA by a man who answered the killer's description. The passenger was bloodied on his hands, sleeves, and the front of his jacket, and was dripping blood onto the bus seat. He had seemed in a daze, proferring 6d (2.5p) for his fare but saying nothing. There were about sixty passengers on the 7.40 pm Number 8 Inner Circle, and some spoke to the man about the blood, but he ignored them. A test on the bus seat revealed Group O blood, identical to Stephanie's, but also the most common group in Britain.

The hunt had been frustrated by the shortage of newspapers over the Christmas Holiday, but now the press helped in the hunt for the bloodstained passenger. The *Sunday Mercury,* the region's largest Sunday paper, published details of the man, saying that he had travelled towards the Ivy Bush on Hagley Road, Edgbaston then round to the northern inner suburbs of Hockley Brook and Aston. The paper appealed for other passengers to come forward, but only a few did. When the dailies reappeared on 27th December the *Daily Express* said "A man with bloodstained hands boarded a crowded bus - dozens saw him, but ignore police appeal", and revealed that every women's hostel and nurses' home in Birmingham was now guarded.

Football crowds were canvassed, Chief Superintendent Jim Haughton appeared in a televised interruption to ATV's *Let's Go* programme in what was probably the first television appeal for information about a crime. Only about ten passengers from the Number 8 appeared and what had seemed a promising clue faded away. The man on the bus was never identified.

Behind the headline stories a great many more routine enquiries, sheer legwork, were going on. An enormous house to house search began, radiating outwards from the hostel, and more than 20,000 adult males were questioned. Because of the holiday, some were not at home when detectives called and had to be visited again. Eventually the operation produced a list of about 300 men who had left their lodgings and not returned after Christmas. Among them was one who had lodged in Islington Row, close to the YWCA Hostel, but Police were unconcerned at his absence because he had given his landlady notice and left a forwarding address in Warrington, Lancs.

An enquiry went to the police in Warrington and the man was asked to call at the police station on 9th February. Detective Sergeant Welborn questioned him about his time in Birmingham, noting that the man seemed upset by some of the questions. After working through the questionnaire supplied by Birmingham, Sergeant Welborn added a question. "Would you have any objection", he asked, "to having your fingerprints taken?"

It was superb bluff, for no fingerprints had been found. A moment of silence followed, then the tubby, curly haired interviewee said, "I want to tell you about the YWCA. I had something to do with that". Jim Haughton's hunt was over.

Patrick Joseph Byrne, known as "Wacky" to his mates, was an Irish labourer who had worked in Birmingham. He appeared before Birmingham Assizes at the Victoria Law Courts on 23rd March 1960 where he pleaded not guilty to murder, despite a lengthy statement made to the Police.

Byrne had told Police of his Peeping Tom activities, and how on 23rd December, he had been near Edencroft and felt like a peep through a window. Seeing only one light in the Annexe, he had peered through the curtain gap and seen a girl in red pullover and underskirt. He then climbed through a window and stood on a chair in the corridor to look through the fanlight over the girl's door hoping that she would undress. When she did not he became "browned off" and was about to leave when she opened the door.

According to the statement, the girl asked what he was doing and was told he was looking for someone. She offered to fetch the Warden and, as she turned, his arm touched her breast. Byrne took hold of her breasts and forcibly kissed her, then thrust her back into the room. There he viciously assaulted and strangled her. With his clothes off, he took a kitchen knife and hacked at the body to remove the head, breaking the knife in the process. The severed head he held up by the hair, looking at it in the mirror. He had left the note because "I wanted everybody to see my life in one little note".

Dressing, he went to the rear of the Annexe, intending to "terrorise all the women. I wanted to get my own back on them for causing my nervous tension through sex". When he saw another light in the washroom he slipped in to attack Margaret Brown with a stone from the garden.

After running away, he went to his lodgings for a thorough wash, talking to himself in the bathroom mirror and looking for signs of insanity. He found none, but wrote to his landlady and fellow lodgers:

> "Dear Mum and Boys, I'm very sorry you'll have
> to receive this horrible letter. Like Jock had two
> personalities I must be the same. One very bad
> and this other one the real me."

Byrne's statement continued that he did not leave the note, but put it in his pocket. He decided on suicide, but "I thought of my mother at Christmas. I didn't want to upset anybody at Christmas so I thought I would put it off until after Christmas".

Mr R.K.Browne QC defended Byrne, argued that his client suffered substantial mental impairment and ask the jury to return a verdict of manslaughter on the grounds of diminished responsibility. However, after three quarters of an hour Byrne was found guilty of murder and sentenced to imprisonment for life.

In the Court of Appeal on 4th July 1960 the conviction was quashed and replaced by a verdict of manslaughter, an offence carrying a maximum penalty of life imprisonment but usually attracts a sentence of about three years. In Byrne's case the sentence was not altered, Lord Chief Justice Parker saying that it was "the only possible sentence, having regard to Byrne's tendencies".

It was eight days short of the 1960s when Stephanie Baird died at the hands of a man who had been haunted by fear and hatred of women since his teens, and had fantasies of sexual violence. The so called permissive society was on the horizon, and whatever its shortcomings, some permissiveness in the upbringing of "Wacky" Byrne might have prevented that sinister Walter Mitty from slithering into his savage dreamworld after a Christmas drinking session, and might have saved the life of Stephanie Baird.

An Application To The Senses
(Nuneaton, Warks 1849)

On 18th May 1849 Thomas Ball went fishing with a friend,
Joseph Petty. They returned in the late afternoon and, later
on the same evening Petty called back at Balls' home.

He was surprised to find Thomas Ball ill, for his friend had
been in good spirits after their fishing trip. So worried was
he that he returned to the Ball's cottage very much later, at
about midnight.

By then Thomas was very ill indeed and complaining of
coldness and numbness in his arms and legs. The doctor was
summoned but, in the small hours of the morning, Tom died.
A death certificate was issued showing the cause of death
as gastritis.

Then the gossip began. Who knows why? Did Mary Ball
seem less than properly grief stricken at her husband's
death. She was said to have remarked to a neighbour that
"It's a good job he's gone". Others recalled her declaring
that, "One of these days I'll poison him", and someone
claimed that Mary had admitted to them that she had poisoned Tom's food.

A post mortem was held on the late Thomas Ball, who
proved (at least, according to the science of the day) to
have died of arsenical poisoning rather than gastritis. His
widow was taken to gaol.

Mary Ball was then in her thirties and still attractive to men.
She had been born one of four daughters of a publican and
became a weaver, as did her sisters. Nuneaton was a town
full of weavers, and when Mary took a husband he was a
weaver too.

Marriage for Mary became a disaster. In twelve years she
bore Tom six children, but only one survived. Keeping her
looks despite her child bearing, she found that far from
appreciating the fact, her drunken, workshy husband grew
insanely jealous of her.

Time after time he accused her of faithlessness. Mary was hot tempered and would answer with spirit. Then Thomas would beat her. Neighbours heard the loud arguments through the years and recalled Mary appearing after them with black eyes and split lips. They did not, of course, intervene; they were English and respected a couple's privacy and a man's right to beat his wife. They were, however, law abiding; they remembered Mary's many declarations that some day she would do for Thomas.

There were no refuges for battered wives one hundred and fifty years ago. Divorce was a costly impossibility for the working class and leaving her vicious lout of a husband would have thrown poor Mary into the workhouse or onto the streets. If she had poisoned her husband, it was a remedy quite often applied by women in her situation. Arsenic was a common substance at the time. In the country it was a regular const-ituent of sheep dips, in the town it was a frequent ingred-ient of insecticides and rat poisons. It could be purchased at any chemist's shop.

The couple's cottage was searched, and a twist of paper containing arsenic was found. Mary said she had bought it to eliminate an infestation of bugs in the cottage and left it on a shelf in the cupboard. Perhaps, she suggested, Thomas had mistaken it for salt and applied it to his gruel. The sugg-estion did not impress her accusers and she was sent for trial.

The trial ended strangely. The foreman of the jury returned a verdict of guilty, adding a recommendation to mercy. It might be hoped that even a Victorian jury could be moved by Mary's story, but that was not the reason for the recomm-endation. Poisoners have always suffered a poor public image. Their planning and secrecy and the sufferings inflicted on their victims add to the simple fact of murder. Mr Justice Coleridge did not want to be hampered in dealing with a poisoner by sentimentality among the jurors and demanded of the foreman why any mercy should be shown to the pris-oner. The foreman explained that it was because some of the jury were not satisfied with some aspects of the evidence.

A verdict, however wrongly founded, had been received in court and the judge should have declared a mistrial and put the case back to be tried again. He did not do so, but ordered the jury back to their room, a clear indication that he expected a proper, hanging, verdict this time with no silly sentiment, and that is what he got.

We do not know what part of the case failed to satisfy the jury. It may have been the scientific evidence. For decades after Mary's trial there were arguments over the analysis of arsenic in human remains and, when the scientific problems were finally solved, the answers made it clear that many people might have suffered wrongful conviction on mistaken evidence.

On the return of that second, illegal, verdict, Mary shrieked her innocence and pleaded for mercy. Judge Coleridge was implacable:

"I cannot hold out to you the least hope of mercy, but the law allows you more time than you allowed your victim whom you sent to his last abode with all his sins upon him. You now have time to repent, and I hope that you will make good use of that time by praying to that just God whom you have so grossly offended."

There was no legal aid and no Court of Appeal to review the illegal behaviour of Mr Justice Coleridge. Mary went to the condemned cell.

Mary Ball was given one week between her sentence and its execution. During that time she saw her family, ate little and frustrated the prison chaplain by refusing to confess.

It might be thought that the function of a Chaplain in a capital case was to offer the consolations of religion to those condemned to die. However, many saw themselves as part of the system of justice, with an obligation to extract confessions that would wipe out any popular impression of injustice and bolster the majesty and infallibility of the law.

The Reverend Richard Chapman was one such, and the jury's unease at the trial would have made a publishable confession particularly necessary. He read scripture to Mary in her cell and prayed at her, but she would not confess. In desperation he declared her "inaccessible to reason" and adopted another approach, which he characterised as an "application to the senses".

Seizing Mary's hand, this ordained representative of the boundless mercy and compassion of God held it in the flame of the candle, asking "Do you feel pain?" She wrenched her hand away, but she did not cry out. She was a woman to whom pain had been a daily presence for years. Chapman begged her to repent and confess, telling her that what she had suffered from the candle was as nothing compared to the pains of hellfire. It was in vain. Mary remained silent.

In the last hours of her life Mary Ball did make a confession. How it was obtained and what it may be worth cannot be judged in the light of Chapman's searing candle. She died before an enormous crowd at Coventry on 9th August 1849 and was buried in the prison, the last woman publicly executed in Coventry.

As gossip had spread after her husband's death, soon it followed in the wake of Mary's; gossip that she had been tortured into a confession. The visiting justices of Coventry Prison suspended the Reverend Mr Chapman.

Cynics may differ, but we do seem to have moved a little into the light since Mary's day. There are now free divorces and refuges for battered wives, there is legal aid for defendants and a Court of Appeal to review the whimsical illegalities of judges. None of these things operates perfectly, but at least we are trying. Chaplains no longer torture confessions from prisoners and we have recognised that the Commandment "Thou shalt not kill" binds the state as well as the citizen, and have done away with the perverted obscenity of the death sentence.

We also have a Parole Board with wide powers to release convicts before they have served their full sentences. It claims that a prisoner's protestation of innocence does not affect their decision but in a recent case the Board justified a refusal of parole on the basis that the prisoner "had not addressed her wrongdoing". I do not understand what that is intended to mean in the case of an innocent person. Perhaps the Reverend Mr Chapman would.

Not many people in these days believe in hellfire, but Mr Chapman did. If it exists, one can hardly help hoping that he spent at least a little time becoming acquainted with the pain of fire.

As Though She Had Disappeared
(West Bromwich, Staffs 1961)

Dorothy Mills' life was so respectable that people might have thought nothing more dramatic would ever occur in it than winning the local Tennis Club championship.

Dorothy lived with her parents in Bernard Street, West Bromwich. At the age of 32 she was single and had been a filing clerk in the Borough Surveyor's office at West Bromwich Town Hall since she left school at 14. Dorothy went to church weekly and had a reputation for being reserved and quiet. She had no known regular boyfriend; apparently her passion was for tennis.

As a member of the town's Wesley Tennis Club in Bratt Street, she played and won regularly. She held a number of trophies and was regarded as one of the Club's best players. Tennis is not, you might think, a dangerous pastime. It does not have the penumbra of crime that accretes to horse racing, boxing or the greyhound track. One does not hear of huge bets on tennis matches, of players being doped or bribed to lose. Even so, it was at Wesley Tennis Club that Dorothy died.

At 6 six o'clock on the evening of Saturday 21st January 1961 Dorothy left her adoptive parents' home for the last time. She told them as she did every Saturday that she would not be late home.

At about 9.45 pm a handbag was found in Sandwell Road near its junction with Hargate Lane and behind the Tennis Club. It was quite close to Dorothy's home, for Bernard Street lay off Hargate Lane. The bag was empty and the £4 or so that Dorothy had with her was missing. At the time no one understood its significance.

Dorothy Mills did not come home on that Saturday night and, at about 6 o'clock the following evening her body was found outside a shed in the Tennis Club grounds. She had been attacked with enormous violence and had fought back vigorously. So fierce had been the assault that her skull was shattered into thirteen pieces.

For such a quiet girl to die by violence one might have thought she had been the victim of some random, senseless attack. The finding of her handbag in Sandwell Road (for it was hers) supported such a theory. Perhaps she had the bad fortune to be seized by a madman as she made her way from home, and dragged into the Tennis Club to meet her death. A coincidence, then, that the champion who spent so much time at the Bratt Street Club should die there? Experienced detectives shudder at the thought of a coincidence, for they rarely happen.

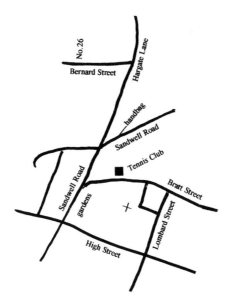

When the inquest assembled the post mortem evidence revealed another possible motive for murder, one that shocked Dorothy's friends and colleagues. At the time of her death she had been thirteen weeks pregnant. Nobody had any idea who the man was.

Detectives on the case, led by Detective Chief Superintendent Frank Tucker and assisted by Scotland Yard, needed answers to two questions. Who was Dorothy's secret lover, and where had she been between leaving home at 6 pm on Saturday and her death about three and a half hours later?

They believed that they were approaching an answer to the first question when a friend of Dorothy's told them that she had often been used as an excuse. Dorothy would claim to be going out with her friend when she was with someone else.

Unfortunately the friend could not say who it was that Dorothy saw on those occasions.

To answer the second question they appealed to the people of West Bromwich to tell them what they knew of Dorothy. They had no useful response. They asked for sightings of her on that evening, but they got none. They broadcast appeals at West Bromwich Albion and Wolverhampton Wanderers football matches, but still no information came. They scoured the Tennis Club grounds with metal detectors and trawled powerful magnets in canals, but no new clues emerged.

After two years they had taken 8,500 statements and still did not know the identity of Dorothy's lover or where she was during the lost hours. Superintendent Tucker said, "It is as though she had disappeared into thin air after leaving her home".

West Bromwich gained a reputation from the case as a town that would not help the police investigations, but it was probably undeserved. January 21st 1961 was a cold, snowy day, and it was after dark when Dorothy left home. It may simply be that on that unpleasant evening nobody saw her except the killer. If she met someone, it is obvious that in such weather they would not have remained out of doors, so they were not necessarily easy to spot. They might have met in his car and sat in it or travelled elsewhere.

Was she killed by a madman for the £4 in her handbag? Probably not. Did she meet someone she knew, perhaps the father of her unborn child, and die when an argument flared into violence? Possibly. Did a calculating killer make a date with her intending to murder her? Maybe. Might there have been something in her handbag that the killer feared would lead to him? Very probably, so that after leaving her dead body he rifled the bag and flung it away as he fled.

She seems to have led a regular, restricted life apart from her anonymous lover. Where in her narrow orbit could she have met him? Was he a member of the Tennis Club or a colleague in the Town Hall? Dorothy was only 32 when she died. Had she lived she would now be in her late 60s Her killer might have been older or younger, but it is quite possible that he is still alive. Perhaps one day someone in the silent town of West Bromwich will speak.

Unsolved murder files stay open indefinitely, but police resources are limited. They must eventually move on to more
fruitful enquiries. The investigation the death of Dorothy
Mills' death is no further forward now than it was more than
thirty years ago, and we may never know the identity of her
killer.

A Shot Rang Out, the Policeman Fell
(Birmingham 1881)

If you want to find out more about the crimes in this collection and others, there is a note about sources at the front
of the book. It is not complete and could not be, for pursuit of the stories of past murders involves accumulating
books, pamphlets, magazine and newspaper cuttings in ever
growing quantities. However, the next case does not come
from a printed source.

When most people were illiterate, newsgatherers and story-
tellers wove their facts and their fictions into verse and
melody to make them more dramatic and memorable. The
ballads they created were intended to be topical, but the
best of them developed a life of their own. The song of
Dick Turpin was sung a century after his death by cow-
boys on the western plains of America, and we know
through ancient verses the stories of the bandits of the
Scottish border.

When printing started in England it was very limited and
expensive. For a hundred years or more, newspapers were
for the well to do, but local printers soon supplied the
need for information on the latest murders. They printed
"broadsides" or "broadsheets", which were single sided
sheets featuring a lurid account of the crime, often illustrated with a woodcut and including a set of verses. Many
of these were the most wretched doggerel (see the coll-
ections in the Birmingham Reference Library and the Salt
Library at Stafford if you don't believe me), but the best
went on to live as folksongs.

In the 1960s Britain was swept by a folk music revival in
which people of all kinds and ages suddenly became interested in the surviving songs of the common people. Night

after night in clubs all over the country singers swapped
songs, and so it was that one night at the Partisan Club in
Birmingham I learned of Jim McCann's crime and its sequel.
This ballad is certainly not doggerel, but thoroughly well
crafted with lively and consistent rhythms, impeccable
rhymes and near perfect scansion.

The Ballad of Jim McCann

Come all you gallant Irishmen and Englishmen as well,
'Tis of a man called Jim McCann, his story I would tell.
He was born and raised in Mayo, but soon was forced to roam,
And following the building trade made Birmingham his home.

In the fierce and bitter winter of the year of '81
McCann he was a slater good, but of work he could get none.
"If I could get to Boston town, if I could raise the fare,
I have two older brothers who are doing well out there".

One night he walked down Fazeley Street, through Henns
                                    Walk and Dale End,
To stay and starve in Birmingham, he no longer did intend,
In a jewellers on the High Street some cash lay in a drawer -
"I reckon that that's owed to me, to even up the score".

He forced the lock, he forced the drawer, his pockets soon were
                                                    lined,
When a passing Policeman spied him through a hole torn in a blind,
McCann he turned and drew a gun as the man came through the door,
"Dont move!" he cried, "Or you'll not see your family any more!"

A shot rang out, the Policeman fell and lay all on the ground,
McCann for New Street Station fled, without once looking round.
From the window of a Liverpool train he flung the gun away
And was on the boat for Boston very early the next day.

We were living in East Boston then, up by Decatur Street,
When a man from Philadelphia my father chanced to meet,
Who said that in that city, with his family by his side,
At the age of only forty-seven, Jim McCann had died.

He died in Philadelphia, so also did his wife,
Working hard for every cent all the days of his short life,
And whether he did right or wrong, I'm not the one to say,
But he owed what life he had at all to the deed he did that day.

The singer from whom I learned the song was an Irish lady who claimed McCann as a relative. She told me that it him had crossed the Atlantic from the American branch of her family, but the crime that it records took place on a cold, dark night in Birmingham's High Street, more than a century ago.

If you want to sing it, the tune I was given is a variant of *Van Diemen's Land,* and the words will fit any similarly structured melody, like *Swansea Barracks* or almost any "Come all ye" air.

The only difficulty with Jim McCann's song is not musical, but a question of fact. A search of the Birmingham newspapers for the period does not reveal any stories about the shooting of a policeman, in the High Street or anywhere else. The West Midlands Police Museum tells me that only three officers were killed in Birmingham during the whole of Queen Victoria's reign. So what did happen? Did McCann shoot at a constable and flee believing he had killed him? Did he merely injure the officer? Did he steal the cash undetected and emigrate and brag to his family in Boston about a crime he never committed?

If any reader can throw any light on this little mystery I shall be delighted to hear from them care of the publisher.

He Was Muttering Some Words
(Tipton, Staffs 1936)

Cox's Bridge crossed the canal at Princes End just where it flowed under Wednesbury Oak Road. This was the Wednesbury Oak Loop, a meander of the old (Brindly) main line of the Birmingham Canal which has since been filled in south of Bradley. On a winter night the area was dark and there were few houses around, though the bridge itself was lit by a single lamp post. Not a place for courting, not on a February night when the ice was crackling across the canal in sheets, but perhaps a place for murder.

On the morning of Saturday 15th February 1936, a gipsy walking the towpath found a corpse in the ice by Cox's Bridge. Recovered from the water, it proved to be the body of a young woman who had been killed by blows to the head from something like a hammer. The police under Bilston's Superintendent Orland did not need to search far for the scene of the murder, for they found a pool of frozen blood 20 yards from Cox's Bridge.

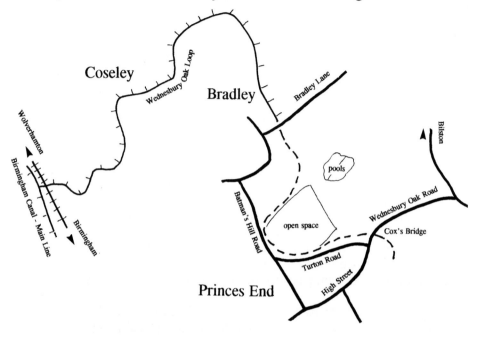

The dead woman was Eliza Jane Worton, known as "Jinny". At 25 years old, she had been married for four years to a naval stoker who had been at sea about eighteen months. Jinny lived with her parents in Phoenix Street, West Bromwich and worked as a breeze ash riddler at Gadd's Forge in Church Lane, Tipton. She was popular with her workmates and was friendly with a lorry driver from Sedgley, William Oakley, whose firm carried ash from Gadd's works. Sometimes he gave her lifts home.

The police considered, briefly, the idea that Jinny was the victim of a road accident and that a driver had panicked and flung the body into the canal, but the nature of her injuries ruled that out. Eliza Jane Worton had been murdered some time late on Saint Valentine's night.

No witnesses to murder could be found, but four people were traced who knew that something strange happened at Cox's Bridge on that Friday night.

A couple leaving the Coach & Horses pub had seen a lorry under the solitary street lamp by the bridge. They thought it an odd place to stop, the more so as they saw the difficulty of a bus driver in manoeuvring his vehicle round the lorry and onto the bridge. Mr and Mrs Stafford lived in the Lock House, along the canal from Cox's Bridge towards Bradley. They told Superintendent Orland's men:

> "We could not see who the driver was, but he did get out of the cab and walk down the bank. He was muttering some words which we were unable to make out."

Better yet were two youths, Sidney Johnson and Harold Southall, who worked at Wainwright's Coal Wharf near the bridge. They too had seen a lorry under the lamp at about 10 o'clock. It had stood there for some ten minutes, and though they had been unable to see if anyone was in the cab, they were both sure that on the door was written, "Oakley, Upper Ettingshall, Coseley", or perhaps "Oakley Brothers". This was the firm owned by William Oakley's brother and for which William drove.

Forty eight hours after the murder another corpse came out of the canal, this time at Eagle Lane, Great Bridge, about a mile and a half from Cox's Bridge. The was the body of a middle aged Tipton man, William Haynes, and gossip linked his death with the murder of Eliza Jane Worton. The police had other ideas. It was said that they had received an anonymous letter identifying the killer but, be that as it may, they had every reason to invite William Oakley to stand on an identification parade at Bilston Police Station.

All four witnesses failed to identify Oakley as the driver of the mysterious lorry. Sidney Johnson and Harold Southall, who had been able to read the inscription on the cab, were taken to Oakley Brothers yard at Ettingshall Road to look over the firm's three Bedford lorries. There they unhesitatingly identified the lorry usually driven by William Oakley. A smear of blood was found on the outside of the cab.

Oakley, who was still a free man, gave an interview to the press at his home in 41 Bilston Street, Sedgley. He told them that he had known Jinny Worton for about a year, but insisted that he had no knowledge of her death. On 14th February he had been nowhere near Wednesbury Oak Road. His lorry had suffered engine trouble that afternoon and evening, and that was why he had arrived back at the firm's yard at about 10.10 that night. His brother Horace had just left the White Horse pub and met him in the yard.

Perhaps he impressed the press and their readers, but he did not impress the police. They were looking into bloodstains found on Oakley's clothing when he was first interviewed. He had tried to conceal them and said that they came from cuts on his hands caused by his job. The police set forensic scientists to work on the stains.

William Oakley was arrested and an inquest on Eliza Jane Worton was opened and adjourned at the Rising Sun pub in Princes End. She was buried in West Bromwich cemetery and a committal court sat under Mayor T Wood.

A Dudley solicitor, Mr Bergendorff, defended Oakley, arguing the circumstantial nature of the case against him. He pointed out that it would be preposterous for anyone to dispose of a body while their vehicle was parked directly under a street lamp with buses going past. Despite Mr Bergendorff's best efforts, Oakley was committed to Stafford Assizes.

When the trial came on in July, William Oakley's defence was led by Norman Birkett, KC. We last came across him as the prosecutor of Alfred Arthur Rouse, twisting the mouthy salesman in the witness box while forcing him to hold onto the damning carburettor, but he was just as able when defending. His forte was cross examination, in which he displayed a fearsome instinct for the right question to ask, or the occasion when no question should be asked.

Stage by stage he destroyed the prosecution's flimsy case. There were no witnesses to the crime, only people who had seen a lorry and not its driver. Birkett pressed Johnson and Southall on their two versions of the name on the lorry.

There was no confession, no dubious comments to police-men as in Rouse's case. There was no scientific evidence, for Oakley's grease sodden working clothing had made analysis of the bloodstains difficult. The best that could be said was that they seemed to be of the same group as the dead woman's blood but could not be definitely spec-ified as such. If there had been a bloodstain on the outside of the cab, there was none inside. Blow by cunning blow, Birkett eroded the Crown's case.

In Oakley's defence Birkett needed to establish little, for the Crown had proved nothing. He called Oakley's mother, Mrs Sarah Grainger, to say that her son had visited her home on Thursday 13th February, the day before the murder, with cuts on his hands, which she had bandaged. Oakley's wife testified that he was a "perfect husband and a perfect father", while his sister Evelyn and his step sister, Olive Grainger, said that he had acted normally on Saint Valentine's night when he came back to the yard. "He was just his normal, cheerful self" said Olive. The driver of the lorry was said to have worn a cap with a shiny peak. Birkett held up Oakley's grubby cap to the jury, showing them that it did not shine under the courtroom lamps.

As he had convicted Rouse, Norman Birkett triumphed again, for the jury acquitted William Oakley, and the Cox's Bridge murder of Jinny Worton stands unsolved to this day.

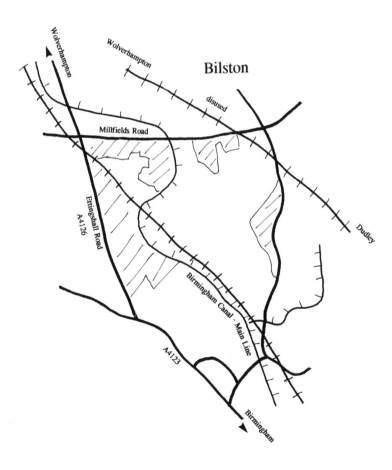

.....And A Last Mystery
(Bilston, Staffs 1914)

What can you make of a murder when you know virtually nothing about the victim, have no idea who killed him or why, and cannot understand why the body was found where it was? To close this selection, let me tell you about an 80 year old case that drove two Chief Constables desperate and was never solved. Personally I believe that it can never now be solved, but if you are very old and wish to confess, or very clever and can work out what happened, please feel free to write to me care of the publisher.

The scene is a piece of waste ground off Millfields Road, Ettingshall in January 1914. It is crossed by a footpath to Wrights Foundry and on its west side is the Birmingham - Wolverhampton railway line and the Main Line of the Birmingham Canal. To the east is the Dudley - Wolverhampton railway, since dismantled. On this land is a circular trench surrounding a low brick wall, which is the top of a ventilator shaft to a disused mine. It is a grey, cold morning with snowflakes blowing in the wind and whitening the ground. At about 8 o'clock two young girls pass along the footpath, heads down in the bitter wind and clutching wrapped basins of cooked food for their fathers at the foundry. They notice a dark shape huddled in the trench by the old shaft, but they ignore it, believing it to be a drunk sleeping off his beer.

A short time later two workmen passed by the bundle in the trench and one turned aside to look. As he rolled it over the pale, bloodstained face of a dead man looked up at him.

The police arrived to begin an enquiry that has never, officially ended. That this was murder was quickly evident. The good looking young man had been shot three times, once in the side of the head, once through the skull and once through the left eye. The weapon appeared to have been a small bore pistol and the cartridges had been flung into the trench.

The dead man was well dressed in a fitted blue serge suit over expensive underwear with a scarf, linen and tie of similar cost, all under a blue plaid overcoat in "naval" style (calf length as worn by naval officers at the time).

He had not apparently been robbed, for his gold watch and silver chain were untouched and £9/2/3d (£9.21p) was in his pockets, a considerable sum in 1914.

An artist's impression of the murdered Kent Reeks as he might have looked in the clothes in which he was found.

In a pocket of the expensive overcoat was something that the police expected would tell them more about the dead man, and perhaps about his death. It was a letter from a Mrs Kent near Manchester, his aunt, and all it established was that his name was Kent Reeks.

When questioned Mrs Kent turned out to know very little about her nephew and could throw no light on his death. The police were back to the start again, seeking a way into the mystery.

They learned that Reeks was born in Australia and had been living in the United States. He had crossed the Atlantic in the liner *Empress of Ireland* and booked into a Liverpool hotel, as had two other men who crossed on the same boat.

While in Liverpool he had impressed the hotel staff as being well off, allowing them to see a large roll of dollars that he carried. He was also seen in the company of two men and two women, but they could not be traced. If the two men had been Kent Reeks' fellow passengers on the *Empress of Ireland* that was no help, for they had vanished and seem to have travelled under false names. On 19th January Reeks mentioned to hotel staff that he was going on a trip, but they could not recall where he intended to go.

That was as much as the Staffordshire Police were ever to discover about the dead man. They found no friends or associates in Britain, let alone in Bilston. They had found no motive for killing him, and believing he had been killed elsewhere and taken to Millfield Road, they found no scene of the murder. They could not even discover what he did for a living.

Colonel the Honourable G Anson, Chief Constable of Staffordshire, was possibly not the cream of his profession. At the time of Reeks' death it was only a few years since Sir Arthur Conan Doyle, creator of Sherlock Holmes, had publicly attacked the Chief Constable over the wrongful conviction of George Edalji in the Great Wyrley cattle maiming case, and had named the criminal where the Colonel's force had failed. No analyst came forward this time to point the way, and Colonel Anson retired with the Reeks murder still unsolved.

In those days police officers regarded an unsolved murder on their patch as a stain on the escutcheon. When Colonel Sir Herbert Hunter became Chief Constable he developed a personal interest in the Reeks case which lasted until his death twenty five years ago.

Colonel Hunter believed that Reeks was murdered late on 19th January, but not in Bilston. He thought that the killer or killers had transported the body to the waste ground by car and that one of them had been familiar with the area. Despite his long musing over the case, Hunter died without arriving at a successful conclusion.

Can it now be done? Can anything be made of the few facts found by the police or by Colonel Hunter's theories? Well, some speculations can reasonably be made. Reeks' lack of an obvious source of income while dressing expensively and flashing rolls of notes suggests that he was some kind of criminal. Maybe the mystery men from America who used false names were also criminals. They may not have been associates of Reeks'. They could well have been two of the scores of conmen and card sharpers who worked the Atlantic liners. Perhaps they saw their fellow passenger as a prospective "mark", lured him to a suitable place, robbed him of his roll and shot him.

Or perhaps the men with false names were Reeks' associates and they had come to England on some joint purpose that brought them from Liverpool to the Midlands. Could it be that Reeks saw them as "marks" and tried to con them, or betrayed them in some way that led them to kill him?

Both of these scenarios are plausible, but neither explains why the body was found where it was. The shaft alongside which it lay was 450 feet deep and flooded to a depth of about 150 feet. If Colonel Hunter was right in believing that the killers, or one of them, knew the area, then they should have known that simply toppling the body over the low wall would guarantee its disappearance for ever. Maybe they were disturbed as they dumped it, but no one came forward to remember people on the waste ground on that snowy night. Was the corpse left there, shot as in a gangland execution with the cartridges beside it, as a warning to someone?

The *Empress of Ireland* on which Reeks (and possibly his killers) travelled, returned across the Atlantic, and in May of 1914 was struck by an ore carrier as she came down the Saint Lawrence river in fog and darkness. She rolled over and sank in minutes, with enormous loss of life. In high summer Britain declared war on Germany and murders were pushed off the front pages. More than eighty years have passed and the case has been almost forgotten. The officers who investigated it are dead; even Lizzie Higgins, who hurried past the corpse with her steaming basin on that freezing morning is gone. The mine ventilator shaft has disappeared and the whole large area of land where it surfaced has quite recently been developed for housing and factories. Only the mystery of Kent Reeks remains, to defy the armchair detective as completely as it defied the professionals.